A REVIEW

OF

MR. NEWMAN'S LECTURES

ON

ROMANISM.

CHARLES WOOD, PRINTER,
Poppin's Court, Fleet Street, London.

A REVIEW

OF

MR. NEWMAN'S LECTURES

ON

𝕽𝖔𝖒𝖆𝖓𝖎𝖘𝖒,

WITH

GENERAL OBSERVATIONS ON THE OXFORD TRACTS,
AND DR. PUSEY'S LETTER TO THE
BISHOP OF OXFORD.

BY

THE REV. C. NEVILE,

Rector of Wickenby, Lincolnshire.

" The rejection of tradition as a rule of faith, was the VITAL PRINCIPLE of the
" Reformation." — HERBERT MARSH, D. D. Bishop of Peterborough.

LONDON:
JAMES RIDGWAY, PICCADILLY.
MDCCCXXXIX.

PREFACE.

Since the following pages were sent to the press, I have read Dr. Pusey's Letter to the Bishop of Oxford, the object of which is to defend the Oxford Tracts and the authors of them against the charge of a tendency to Romanism. Dr. Pusey certainly shows that some passages have been misunderstood, and others unfairly treated; and he perhaps justly complains of the errors and inconsistencies of many of his opponents. As an argumentative discourse to prove the point at issue, I think it is a failure; and as it is put forward with this avowed object by the most able man of the party, this very failure must tend to confirm the previous impression with regard to the Popish tendency of these Tracts. It is evidently a careful and elaborate explanation of many supposed objectionable passages; numerous references and quotations are made, particularly to the writings of Mr. Froude and Mr. Newman. How has it happened that the strongest and most remarkable expressions, showing a Popish tendency in those writings, have never been alluded to? In a defence of this kind, why have those passages been left unexplained, which most needed explanation? When general accusations are brought against a work or a party, a great number are in all probability unfounded: where this Popish tendency appears so manifest, it is a natural consequence that it should often be suspected where it does not in reality exist. But when a deliberate and laborious attempt is made to disprove these charges, a defence is worth very little which is limited to these equivocal points. It is surprising that such passages as the following, which we meet with in Mr. Froude, are entirely overlooked and omitted in Dr. Pusey's letter.

"That odious Protestantism." " Really " I hate the Reformation and the Reform- " ers more and more." " As to the Re- " formers, I think worse and worse of " them." " Jewell was what you would " call in these days an irreverent Dis- " senter." How can such expressions as these have escaped Dr. Pusey's attention? Be it remembered that they are not the wild effusions of Mr. Froude. He was "a downright speaker;" his words are to be taken "more literally than those "of other men," and his sentiments are openly adopted by his editors. Amongst the numerous passages in Mr. Froude's writings tending to Popery, Dr. Pusey has not explained or defended one of any consequence. Again, Mr. Newman asserts that *we* hold the *infallibility* of the Church, and that any doctrine is necessarily true *because the Church teaches it.* Is it possible, that in such an undertaking as Dr. Pusey's, such strong, plain, and unequivocal expressions could have been forgotten?

The letter itself seems to be an effort to show how near to Popery a member of the Anglican Church can approach without being compelled to quit it. Whenever our formularies or articles leave an opening it is eagerly seized upon; every dubious passage is strained to the utmost; the Protestant spirit, which is the life and foundation of our Church, in which the Reformation can alone find a justification, is entirely set aside. As an example of this, Dr. Pusey most unfairly evades the twenty-first article, which is in itself sufficient to overthrow the whole doctrine of Church Authority, as put forward by this party. The article declares that " General Councils may err, and some-" times have erred, even in things per-" taining unto God," and the reason given is, " forasmuch as they be an assembly " of men, whereof all be not governed " with the Spirit and Word of God." Dr. Pusey says—

" We believe that, although Councils, " which have been *termed* General, or "which Rome has claimed to be so, have "erred, no real œcumenical Council ever "did." It is clear that this evasion is necessary to reconcile a belief in Church Infallibility with continuing a member of the Anglican Church. When the framers of the Articles used the expression "General Councils," it is impossible they could mean Councils which they themselves denied to be General: then does Dr. Pusey maintain, that what he calls Œcumenical Councils were composed of men who were "all governed "with the Spirit and Word of God?" Can he conceive that the long and fierce contention at Nice could have ever taken place, had this been the case? Some idea may be formed of the manner in which our plainest and most simple articles can be wrested from their true and ordinary sense to admit of this " tendency " to Romanism."

Dr. Pusey argues, that because it is not Popish to use the cross in baptism, it cannot be so " for any privately to retrace " that mark upon himself." This is plausible enough at first sight, and it can be granted that there is no difference in principle in the two cases; but is there none in the practice? If the practice of the Anglican Church has been to use the sign of the cross in one instance and *not* in another, is it not a symptom of a departure from that Church to depart from her practice? There can be no difference in *principle* between the use of a surplice and an embroidered garment: neither the one nor the other is necessarily connected with any theological opinion or doctrine; but if an individual or a party are suspected of holding Popish tenets, it would be a great confirmation of that suspicion to find that they, in their clerical dress, assimilated themselves to the practice of the Romish Church. Besides, Popery may consist in *degree* as well as in *kind*. The Romish Church not only corrupted the pure doctrines of Christianity, but she overloaded and obscured them by a multiplicity of forms and ceremonies: at the Reformation there was a correction of both errors, and it may be Popish to use the sign of the cross twenty times, when it is *not* Popish to use it once; it may be Popish to fast every Friday in the year, and *not* Popish to fast on Good Friday only; it may be Popish to hold saints' days in such superstitious veneration as to continue with laborious ingenuity to date every preface and every letter upon one of them, and *not* Popish to recal them to our remembrance when they occur.

Upon the Celibacy of the Clergy, Dr. Pusey says it has been "*dropped inci-*"*dentally*" by the Oxford Tracts writers, " not systematically promoted." This accords very curiously with Mr. Froude's notion of " infusing principles into the " mind against the reader's will." Dr. Pusey's opinions on the subject are evidently leaning to the Popish view of it. Our Articles leave it quite open. Our Church neither recommends one state of life nor the other to her clergy. What therefore can Dr. Pusey mean when he says, " why require that all his warriors " should cumber themselves with the concerns of this life?"

" Why again should the daughters of

" our land be in a manner *forced* into
" marriage, as in the former days of Ro-
" manism they were into celibacy?"
Where are the clergy *required* to marry,
or the daughters of our land *forced* into
marriage? There is no occasion to invent an evil for the sake of pretending to find a remedy. But Dr. Pusey does not quite leave the matter open. He speaks of celibacy as " a more excellent " way," and thereby departs from the spirit and the practice of the Anglican Church. The passages quoted from Scripture in favour of celibacy applied to the clergy under far different circumstances; they were at that time itinerant ministers, persecuted on all sides, and a wife and family would have been a great hindrance to their due performance of the duties they had to undertake. The

same expressions in Scripture may apply to missionaries from our own Church, but certainly not to the parochial clergy. So far from celibacy being a " more excellent way," I believe not only that married clergymen *are* cæteris paribus the best parochial ministers, but that the very circumstance of their being married enables them to be so. A married clergyman has much greater inducement to remain at home than a single man. That entire devotion to our duty which requires no relaxation is very desirable, but it cannot be obtained except in a very few cases, and it is much better that we should find our pleasures at home than have to seek them abroad. Again, the usefulness of a parochial minister in a great measure depends upon the light in which he is regarded, and the manner in which he is received by his parishioners, and I would ask whether the married or the single life is the greatest recommendation to them? Which is the best introduction to the domestic circle or the sick bed? In visiting the fatherless and the widows in their affliction, is there no advantage in being a husband and a father? Are we not more likely thereby to be able to administer advice or consolation? There is another consideration which ought to prevent any *recommendations* of celibacy as a more " excellent " way." Suppose a hundred young men are persuaded, first, that they ought to devote themselves *entirely* to their profession, and secondly, that a life of celibacy will best enable them to do so,—suppose (and the most limited knowledge of the world will justify the supposition), suppose, I say, that *even one* instance of misconduct occurs in this great number, is not the sin, and the shame, and the scandal of that one single failure more than sufficient to counterbalance the " more excellent way" of all the rest? Dr. Pusey speaks of voluntarily " *fore-* " *going*" blessings, but what virtue is there in such foregoing of them? If the using of them is innocent, why should we reject them? If they are *freely* offered, why should they not be *freely* accepted? Had we not better show to our parishioners what is the due and proper mode of enjoying and using them? Is not the "*foregoing*" those blessings, which God in his mercy has offered to us, something like that *will worship* so notorious in the Romish Church? Is it not quite opposed to the spirit of the Reformed Protestant

Anglican Church? Again, few single clergymen, however circumspect they may be, escape through life the suspicion of irregular conduct: such suspicions, however unfounded, are most detrimental to the usefulness of a parochial minister. Altogether nothing can be more dangerous, inexpedient, or unnecessary than recommending celibacy as a " more ex-" cellent way" to young men just taking orders, who are alike ignorant of the world and of themselves. Nothing can be more rash than to induce them, by any unwarranted praises of celibacy, to embark in a course of life which they would not naturally have chosen for themselves. Nothing can be more cruel and unjust to them than to impress upon them, that they are in any way called upon to renounce the blessings Providence has intended for their use. Dr. Pusey considers the Reformation in the same light in which all his party are compelled to regard it, *viz.* as " simply denying the " undue authority" of the Bishop of Rome. The Reformation was a great deal more than that; it was a casting off the erroneous doctrines and superstitious practices with which the whole Church was more or less infected. The unwillingness with which the members of our Church relinquished these errors, is a sufficient proof that they were not wholly to be attributed to this undue authority exercised over them. It is notorious that they preserved the errors long after they disclaimed the authority; and when the errors themselves were corrected, it cannot be supposed that the *sincere* reformers could have every expression in our articles and liturgy as they wished. It is natural to expect that the traces of Popery would be left behind in a few dubious words, or equivocal sentences. Such instances may, it is true, be discovered, but the sense of the Church is sufficiently known upon them to render their alteration or erasure in *her* judgment unnecessary: I am quite willing to sacrifice my private opinion to that judgment, but the Oxford Tracts writers cannot be allowed to lead us back to Popery by means of a strained interpretation of these particular expressions.

The concluding part of Dr. Pusey's letter is curious enough. It is well known that all the Romish clergy hail these Tracts and their authors with the greatest delight and satisfaction. They ridicule the puny censures which are contained in them. They are acute enough to see that all is granted to them which they need ask. The only principle worth contending for is surrendered to them; a little time and patience will, and must, sweep away the trifling differences *in detail*. Dr. Pusey, on the contrary, would wish to persuade us that his party is the only one of which the Romanists are really afraid; that the ground they take is the only ground on which the battle of the Anglican Church can be successfully fought, and that the Romanists themselves are well aware of it, and that in consequence the Oxford Tracts are regarded by them with the greatest hostility and fear. Dr. Pusey may have imposed upon himself, but he cannot surely so far impose upon his readers. The last remark I shall make upon this letter is, that it contains most prominently the same feature with all the writings of this party, *viz.* the total absence, as Bishop Watson calls it, of the *suspicion of fallibility*. This is the *popery of opinion*, that confident persuasion that *we must* be right, and all who differ from us *must* be wrong, which is the foundation of all the errors of the Romish Church. Pusey and Newman and Keble and Froude all recognize the hand of Providence in what they write or do. If what they preach is rejected, that is a mark of its truth; if on the contrary their opinions spread, this success is a proof of the purity of their doctrine. In short, under whatever circumstances or whatever course of events, the Anglican *must* be the true Church, and their views *must* truly represent what her doctrines are. It is consoling to those who differ from them, and who still respect the authority of their Church, and doubt their private judgment—it is consoling indeed to reflect that such men as Tillotson, Watson, Law, and Paley, were totally opposed to their peculiar tenets. It is a proud satisfaction for that party, so contemptuously termed " mere Pro-" testants," to reflect that men of the most superior talents, the most extensive learning, the most unblemished piety, have at various times devoted their lives to the defence and propagation of entirely opposite principles, and that many of the most able champions of Christianity have maintained that the Bible, and the Bible only, is the rule of faith.

A REVIEW,

&c &c.

It has appeared to a party at Oxford, composed of men in great reputation for their learning and piety, that there is now only " a comparatively small remnant who fol- " low the ancient doctrines and customs of " our Church, who hold to the creeds and " sacraments, keep from novelties, and are " regular in their devotions, and are what " is sometimes called in reproach *orthodox*." (Introduction to Newman's Lectures on Romanism and Popular Protestantism.) With the praiseworthy intention of recalling the majority, who have so far wandered from the right path, to the proper principles of their Church, they have put forth a series of publications, under the appropriate title of " Tracts for the Times." They have fastened upon that majority the name of " Mere Protestants, or Ultra Protestants :" their religion is called " Popular Protestantism," and an attempt is made to prove that their doctrines are not only incorrect and false, but completely at variance with those of the Church of England. Quotations are brought forward from the writings of some of our leading divines since the Reformation to support this accusation. It is earnestly hoped, perhaps, that this majority, lay and clerical, should see, if not confess, the error of their ways, and gratefully accept the assistance which is offered to them in retracing their steps. However desirable such a consummation may appear to be, it is not much to be expected. As long as human nature remains what it is, as long as the faculty of reason is continued to us, even in its present state of imperfection, some process of conviction must necessarily precede a great change of opinion.

A minority may be carried away or silenced by superior numbers, but the majority will rarely if ever give way to " a small remnant," without the strongest reasons and the plainest arguments being adduced for their doing so. A great schism has in consequence arisen, and the cause of Popular Protestantism has been taken up in several quarters. Attempts have been made to show, so far from the imputations upon the Mere Protestants being just, that *they* continue their adherence to the doctrines and principles of their Church, and that the writers of the Oxford Tracts are the wandering party. They are charged with advocating opinions and putting forward doctrines materially differing from those of the reformed Church of England, and approximating, in a very great degree, to those of the Church of Rome.

It is easy to hold out the danger of controversy and the duty of unity, particularly in these times and under present circumstances, and it is obvious enough that divisions amongst ourselves will not assist us in our defence against our common enemies. But must these considerations induce the majority of the members of the Established Church of this country to yield their judgment and conviction to the minority? Can the writers of the Oxford Tracts so deceive themselves as to suppose that the contest they have originated is between intellect and numbers, learning and ignorance, or zeal and indifference? Do they suppose a *catena patrum*, containing a few expressions from the writings of *some* of our most able and excellent divines, favourable to their particular views, is to place the correctness of those views beyond a doubt? They have had before this time the opportunity of studying a *catena patrum* containing sentiments rather different to their own, which they had overlooked in their researches. Mr. Moore Capes has given them extracts from Ridley, Tindal, Frith, Barnes, Nicholas Ridley, Latimer, Cranmer, Bradford, Hooper, Rogers, Turner,

Jewell, Parker, Hooker, Herbert, Chillingworth, Usher, Hall, Taylor, Reynolds, Pearson, Hopkins, Tillotson, Stillingfleet, Burnet, South, Whitby, Gibson, Butler, Secker, Sherlock, Horsley, and Tomline, which are diametrically opposed to the doctrines they are so anxious to propagate. They have eagerly caught at what appears to afford them episcopal sanction in their own times. The Bishop of Oxford's charge has been to them a grateful testimony of the approbation of their Diocesan, which, on their own principles, must be of inestimable value. A justification pronounced *ex Cathedrâ*, where every word must have been well weighed and deliberated upon, to say nothing of their high notions of Church authority, overwhelms all the objections of their brother ministers at once in their sight. Let us examine this justification. What are the expressions of the Bishop of Oxford upon the subject? " You will probably expect that I should " say something of that *peculiar develop-*

"*ment of religious feeling in one part of the diocese,* of which so much has been said, and which has been supposed to tend immediately to a revival of several of the errors of Romanism. In point of fact I have been continually (though anonymously) appealed to in my official capacity to check breaches both of doctrine and discipline, through the growth of Popery among us. Now, as regards the latter point, breaches of discipline namely, on points connected with the public services of the Church, I really am unable, after diligent inquiry, to find any thing which can be so interpreted. I am given to understand, that an injudicious attempt was made in one instance, to adopt some forgotten portion of the ancient clerical dress; but *I believe* it was speedily abandoned, and I do not think it likely we shall hear of a repetition of this, *or similar indiscretions.* At the same time, so much of what has been objected to has arisen from minute atten-

" tion to the Rubric; and I esteem unifor-
" mity so highly (and uniformity can never
" be obtained without strict attention to
" the Rubric) that I confess I would rather
" follow an antiquated custom (even were
" it so designated) *with* the Rubric, than
" be entangled in the modern confusions
" which ensue from the neglect of it.

" With reference to errors in doctrine,
" which have been imputed to the series of
" publications called the 'Tracts for the
" Times,' it can hardly be expected that on
" an occasion like the present, I should
" enter into, or give a handle to any thing
" which might hereafter tend to controver-
" sial discussions. Into controversy I will
" not enter. But, generally speaking, I
" may say, that in these days of lax and
" spurious liberality, any thing which tends
" to recal forgotten truths is valuable; and
" where these publications have directed
" men's minds to such important matters as
" the union, the discipline, and the autho-
" rity of the Church, I think they have done

" good service; but there may be some
" points in which perhaps, from *ambiguity
" of expression,* or similar causes, it is not
" impossible but that evil, rather than the
" intended good, may be produced on minds
" of a peculiar temperament. I have more
" fear of the disciples than of the teachers.
" In speaking, therefore, of the authors
" and Tracts in question, I would say, that
" I think their desire to restore the ancient
" discipline of the Church most praise-
" worthy; I rejoice in their attempts to
" secure a stricter attention to the Rubrical
" directions in the Book of Common Prayer;
" and I heartily approve of the spirit which
" would restore a due observance of the
" fasts and festivals of the Church; *but I
" would implore them,* by the purity of their
" intentions, to be cautious, both in their
" writings and actions, to take heed lest
" their good be evil spoken of; *lest in their
" exertions to re-establish unity, they un-
" happily create fresh schism; lest in their
" admiration of antiquity, they revert to*

"*practices which heretofore have ended* "*in superstition.*"—(Bishop of Oxford's Charge, July, 1838.)

We must remember that this supposed episcopal approbation comes from their own Bishop: we may naturally conclude he would speak as favourably as he could of the clergy in his own diocese; he would avoid any appearance of censure if possible. Under all these strong and favourable circumstances, surely the quotation I have given must be regarded as very equivocal commendation: there is first an admission that this is "a peculiar development of feel- "ing in one part of the diocese," that diocese being one of a great number into which our Church is divided, the word *peculiar* stamps the views of this party as particular or uncommon, and they are acknowledged to be confined to a very small section of our Church. A hint is thrown out, that from " ambiguity of expression" or " simi- "lar causes," evil may be produced instead of good; and the Bishop dismisses the subject by "*imploring*" them to be cautious, "lest in their exertions to re-establish unity, "they unhappily create fresh schism; lest "in their admiration of antiquity, they re-"vert to practices which heretofore have "ended in superstition." There can be no doubt that a great majority of the clergy, and an immense majority of the laity of the Anglican Church (which is the new expression for the obsolete Church of England) consider that this party *have* created fresh schism, and *have* in their admiration for antiquity " reverted to practices which " heretofore have ended in superstition ;" and to meet the Oxford Tracts on their own grounds, giving full latitude to their " peculiar" doctrines upon Church authority, we have episcopal sanction for our opinion: we have the sentiments of another Bishop, delivered under the same circumstances, and certainly expressed in much more unequivocal terms. The Bishop of Chester says, " One subject more espe-" cially concerns the Church at present;

"because it is daily assuming a more se-
"rious and alarming aspect, and threatens
"a revival of the worst evils of the Romish
"system. Under the specious pretence of
"deference to antiquity, and respect for
"primitive models, the foundations of our
"Protestant Church are undermined by
"men who dwell within her walls, and
"those who sit in the Reformers' seat are
"traducing the Reformation."—(Bishop of Chester's Charge.)

Has not therefore the large party in our Church at least as much right to publish their sentiments as the smaller party? If schism does arise from the discussion so created, is it fair to charge it all upon one side?—Certainly not. Heavy complaints have however been made against the "Mere Protestant Party" on this account. They have been accused of wilfully misunderstanding or misrepresenting the true sentiments of the writers of the Oxford Tracts, and of having founded most uncharitable censures upon such misrepresentation.

Many comments have been made upon ignorant and unlearned individuals presuming to argue the question against such an array of talents and learning: as an example I quote the following from Dr. Hook's notes to his visitation sermon, preached at Ripon:—

"The want of information betrayed by "these accusers, discreditable as it is, is "still more offensive when it is found, as "too frequently is the case, accompanied "with a want of candour, and a tone of "insult towards those whom they cannot "or will not understand. An instance of "this may be given in a work just adver"tised, under the title of 'Revelation not "Tradition." This title is evidently as"sumed to imply that the advocates of the "English Reformation elevate tradition "above the Bible, or that they place tra"dition on an equality with it—thereby "assuming a gross and uncharitable false"hood." In another note he says, "Their "popularity will increase, since their ar-

"guments are not answered, or their statements refuted; they are opposed simply by railing. And those who judge of such things only by second-hand reports, and garbled quotations, and anonymous misrepresentations, will, of course, rail on."

The quotations which have been given in these " anonymous misrepresentations,' are so extraordinary, as coming from any member, not to say minister, of the Established Church, that I have examined the originals in every case which I have met with, and in no one single instance did I find the slightest mistake. Dr. Hook can know little of the Tracts, or the writers of them, or he could never have fallen into the error of terming them " Advocates of English Reformation." It is an odd mode of advocating the Reformation to express increasing hatred against it. Lessons of charity are better enforced by example than by precept, and Dr. Hook's language is not calculated to effect much in that way. It is possible that the party in question may, by their extraordinary avowals, their contradictory statements, and their ambiguous expressions, have drawn some portion of censure upon themselves which they do not deserve.

To enable any candid person to judge how justly the want of charity can be charged by Dr. Hook upon Dr. Shuttleworth, I quote the following from the book referred to:—

"With regard to the authors of these "publications and discourses, I wish to "speak of them, so far as I am acquainted "with them personally, or by common re-"port, with all the respect that they justly "deserve, for their admitted learning, their "talents, and the purity and holiness of "their lives. But I cannot, nor do I wish "to conceal my opinion, that the doctrines "which they advocate, should they become "popular, would in other hands be essen-"tially injurious to the cause of pure Pro-"testantism, and with it, to sound Chris-"tianity, in this country." "In this case, "the respectability of the advocates must "not make us blind to the danger likely "to ensue from the principles which they "adopt."—(Shuttleworth's Not Tradition, but Revelation).

Such is the spirit in which this book is written; and to show how far the author was justified in his opinion of the sentiments of the writers of the Oxford Tracts, he gives numerous extracts from Mr. Froude's Remains, published by this very party, and himself one of the contributors to these tracts. It has been said to be very unjust to lay hold of expressions here and there in any one of these Oxford Tract writers; that they did not mean exactly what they appear to mean; that no person who does not know them can fairly judge of them; that it is only their strong and forcible manner of expressing themselves; that when Mr. Froude (for instance) said he "hated" the Reformation, he only must be understood to imply that he did not approve of it in every particular, &c. Now it matters nothing what he really thought, or what his friends supposed he thought; the only question is what his *readers* would think his opinion was: the effect produced will depend upon that; and I would ask, whether an individual, or any number of individuals, can undertake to instruct an immense body of persons in the proper tenets of their own Church, who are capable of expressing themselves in such a manner? The simplicity required to receive the teaching could never discern that " *hate*" means only " not wholly approve."

It has in the second place been observed, that the particular opinions of an individual contributor to these tracts can not justly be said to apply to the tracts themselves, as they are published by several persons jointly; but whatever affects the credit of one of these editors, must surely attach to any work in which they may have been engaged. If the individuals are not Protestants, the body cannot be so; if each person separately, or even one or two of them, can be proved to hold tenets entirely opposed to those of the Established Church, no joint publication can be looked upon as favourable to it. About Mr. Froude there can indeed be no doubt; and I shall endeavour to show that the sentiments of Mr. Newman are just as anti-Protestant, or his language as ambiguous and exceptionable as Mr. Froude's. I *may* mistake Mr. Newman's meaning in the chief passages: it will be for the candid reader to judge whether the fault is his or mine. If he does not mean what he says, I cannot plead guilty to the charge of misrepresentation or mistake. I can promise that I will not endeavour, from any party spirit, to fasten upon any expressions a stronger sense than his language will fairly bear.

It is my intention to take passage after passage in Mr. Newman's book, and to endeavour to prove from them, that the tenets and principles advanced in it are *not* those of the Anglican Church; or that if they are, the Reformation was a reformation in name only, not in principle; and on this supposition the great majority of the clergy and laity, now attached to the Church of England, can continue in her communion only from mistaking her real doctrines. I shall also endeavour to show, that no idea of a Church can be maintained on Mr. Newman's principles; that so far from his having " realized" the doctrines of the Church of England, which have never been " realized" before, he has conceived a notion of a *via media*, which can exist only in the imaginations of a few enthusiastic individuals, who being educated as Protestants, and having to a certain extent relapsed into Popery, have formed a confused theory upon the subject of Church Authority; or to take Mr. Newman's simile, a sort of grey, between black and white, neither belonging to one side or the other: his attempt to establish such a theory has been attended with a perpetual series of contradictions; one line granting all the Pope himself would ask, another all the most zealous " mere Protestant" would require; one argument proving the " infallibility of the Church," another disproving it; one position advanced, which can only be so advanced by exercising the right of private judgment; another, the foundation of which must be the denial of that right. There are inferences in the place of arguments, assumptions instead of evidence, and parallels instead of proofs. It is however no reflection upon Mr. Newman's talents if he has failed in establishing the points he is so desirous of doing. The fault is in the cause, not in the advocate. He has attempted impossibilities; all his efforts are directed to support a system of theology which no human ingenuity would enable him to do. I wish we could have Church Infallibility, with its many advantages, and without its deplorable and inevitable evils; or the unlimited right of private judgment with the certainty that individuals would invariably embrace truth and reject error; but the attainment of either is equally hopeless. Our choice may be at best a choice of evils, but choose we must: we cannot have a grey compound between the two, combining the advantages, and avoiding the disadvantages of each. We cannot allow the Church to be infallible in *one* doctrine, and fallible in *another;* we cannot allow an appeal to the Scriptures, with the proviso that the Church is to be the sole *interpreter* of them. The right of private judgment is of no avail, if it is limited to one conclusion only. Desirable as it might be to effect this, it is beyond the power of man's intellect; and I think it will appear that the attempt has involved Mr. Newman in all the contradictions and inconsistencies alluded to.

" Surely life is not long enough to
" prove every thing which may be made
" the subject of proof; and, though in-

"quiry is left partly open in order to try
" our earnestness, yet it is in a great mea-
" sure, and in the most important points,
" superseded by Revelation, which dis-
" closes things which reason could not
" reach, saves us the labour of using it
" when it might avail, and sanctions the
" *principle* of dispensing with it in all
" cases."

Can any Papist ask more than such an admission?

" As might be expected, then, we have
" succeeded in our attempt; we have suc-
" ceeded in raising clouds which effec-
" tually hide the sun from us, and we
" having nothing left but to grope our way
" by our reason as we best can — our
" necessary, because now our only guide."

In the latter proposition surely any mere Protestant may find his justification. If " reason is our only guide," we may at least follow our own, in preference to that of other people; at all events we may choose whose reason we will follow. We may take the Pope, the Archbishop of Canterbury, or the oldest and most respected of the Scotch Presbytery. As I cannot make a single objection to this admission of Mr. Newman's, so am I equally unable to make the matter more clear by any explanation.

Let us examine the first proposition. Because Revelation " discloses things " which reason could not reach," does it necessarily follow that it " saves us the " labour of using it when it might avail, " and sanctions the *principle* of dispensing " with it in all cases?" If it does, where is the man bold enough to attack the Infallibility of the Church? But it is incumbent on Mr. Newman to establish his doctrine before it is necessary for his opponents to try to overthrow it. We cannot be content with assumptions, and speculations, and surmises, and inferences, and then be called upon to prove beyond a doubt that they are untrue. The *onus probandi* rests entirely upon his party.

So far from **Revelation** superseding **Reason** in **Mr. Newman's** sense, every conclusion we can draw from the Scripture history would seem to establish the contrary. How could the Jews or the Gentiles receive the religion of our Saviour, if their reason was to be dispensed with? How could they judge of his pretensions? Why did he work so many miracles to support his teaching, except an appeal was to be made to their reason? How were they to distinguish between him and the " false " Christs and false prophets" which were to arise? How are we, in this our day, to discern between the respective truth of the Christian and the Mahomedan religion? to say nothing of the numerous sects into which Christianity is divided? What can be the use of **Mr. Newman's** book? How can he hope that his " small remnant" are to recover the wandering majority? In short, how is the idea of religion to be kept up if reason is to be *dispensed with?* Reason must judge whether a professed revelation is a revelation or not, or whether the doctrine of any Church is according to Scripture or contrary to it: this is quite different from clearly comprehending the doctrines revealed. We may be capable of ascertaining whether the doctrine of the Trinity is or is not to be found in Scripture, without being at all able to understand such a doctrine when we have found it. The notion that Revelation sanctions the *principle* of dispensing with reason in all cases, is a most gratuitous assumption, without one single argument to support it. Such a proposition involves a contradiction fatal to itself: we never can be *convinced* that our reason is *superseded*, or *dispensed* with; and conviction must precede belief. *Belief* in a doctrine, is only another term for expressing *conviction of the truth of it.*

Besides all this, suppose for a moment that our Saviour, when he revealed his religion to us, intended to dispense with our reason even in all cases, how does that justify a body of Ecclesiastics of any age in calling themselves the Church, assuming their own infallibility, and then dispensing with the reason of the rest of their fellow Christians? And if Mr. Newman's proposition does not mean this, it means nothing of any use to Church Authority: it cannot otherwise at all affect the question whether every private Christian is bound to believe any doctrine " because the Church teaches it," or not.

" We stigmatize it as a bondage to be
" bid take for granted what the wise, the
" good, and the many have gone over and
" determined long before, or to submit to
" what Almighty God has revealed."

Who does Mr. Newman mean by "we?" How dare he assert that any body of Christians, either belonging to the Established Church or the Dissenters, think it "a bond-
" age to submit to what Almighty God has
" revealed," merely because they refuse to allow him or his party, or his Church, to dictate to them what *is* revealed? It is

c

not easy for us, if we ever so much wished it, to " take for granted what the wise, " the good, and the many have determined " long before," when it is beyond all doubt that the wise, and the good, and the many have unfortunately determined upon the most contradictory doctrines. The History of the Church shows us Father against Father, Council against Council, and Century against Century. What was orthodoxy in one age was heresy in the next; the same opinions and tenets which procured the holders of them dignity and credit at one time, brought them to the stake at another.

The wise and the good have been so mixed up with the unwise and the bad, that it is a difficult thing to distinguish them. Amongst the multitude of determinations which we are bid to take for granted, a great number have been arrived at by any thing rather than conscientious conviction. How are we to separate them? If we had followed the wise, the good, and the *many*, we must inevitably have remained Roman Catholics; the Reformation could only have originated in *the few* deserting and separating from *the many*.

"The true voice of Revelation has been "overpowered by the more clamorous tra- "ditions of men; and where there are "rivals, examination is necessary, even "where piety would fain have been rid "of it."

Here we must agree; but by whom is this examination to be made? Mr. Newman thinks by the Anglican Church: that she is to examine into the respective claims of herself, the Romish Church, and the other Protestant Churches; and having decided that she is right, and all the rest mistaken, she has only to communicate this decision to the private Christian, who is to receive her particular doctrines as from infallible authority, or be considered a sinner and a schismatic. Unfortunately for the private Christian, the Church of Rome has decided that *she* is the infallible

Church, and that if he embrace the doctrines of the Anglican Church, he becomes a heretic and a sinner. Supposing true doctrine to be the object sought, is it more likely to be obtained by an examination into the claims of these two Churches, than by consulting the Scriptures themselves? If every private Christian is bound to accept the doctrines of the Church in which he finds himself, the Reformation was founded in the violation of that rule; we could otherwise never have had any Reformation at all.

"The great mass of educated men are
"at once uneasy, impatient, and irritated,
"not simply incredulous, directly they are
"promised from any quarter some clear
"view of the original and apostolic doc-
"trine, to them unknown, on any subject
"of religion."

It cannot be otherwise when this very mass of men, educated and uneducated, have been for centuries grossly imposed upon by a body of ecclesiastics, calling themselves an infallible Church. Is it to be expected, that having just obtained some light after so long a period of darkness inflicted by this Church, they should abandon that light? Is it reasonable that after having received the doctrines of transubstantiation, penance, and worship of images, amongst a variety of others on the authority of their Church, simply " because the Church taught them," they should sacrifice their right of private judgment to another Church on the very same principle?

They may surely be excused a little uneasiness and impatience upon the subject; and this uneasiness and impatience are not likely to be diminished by the consideration that this view of Infallible Authority is supported by a very small section of this other Church; by a party who commence by avowing themselves to be only " a small remnant of it."

" It does not follow then, that doctrines " are uninfluential, when plainly and

" boldly put forward, because they offend
" the prejudices of the age at first hearing.
" Had this been true, Christianity itself
" ought not to have succeeded; and it
" cannot be imagined that the respectable
" and serious men of this day, who express
" concern at what they consider the ex-
" aggerated tone of certain writers on the
" subject of the Church, are more startled
" and offended than the outcasts to whom
" the Apostles preached in the beginning.
" Truth has the gift of overcoming the
" human heart, whether by persuasion or
" by compulsion, whether by inward ac-
" ceptance or by external constraint; and
" if what we preach be truth, it must be
" natural, it must be seasonable, it must
" be popular; it will make itself popular.
" It will find its own. As time goes on,
" and its sway extends, those who thought
" its voice strange and harsh at first, will
" wonder how they could ever so have
" deemed of sounds so musical and thrill-
" ing."

I hope this parallel between the **Oxford** Tracts writers and the Apostles on the one hand, and the respectable and serious men and the outcasts to whom the Apostles preached, on the other, is a little overstrained. The majority of any Church cannot hear such a parallel from the minority without some " impatience and un-" easiness," if not irritation. The Roman Catholic religion certainly overcame the human heart, either by " persuasion or " inward acceptance;" and where *they* failed, by " compulsion and external constraint;" it became " natural," and " sea-" sonable" and " popular," and it " found " its own" in greater numbers than any other creed can ever expect to do. As time went on, and its sway extended, those who " thought its voice strange and harsh " at first, wondered how they could ever " so have deemed of sounds so musical " and thrilling." It had all Mr. Newman's accompaniments of truth. Was it true? If it was, some of the articles of the

Church to which Mr. Newman professes to belong must be false.

Our reformed Church has now existed about three hundred years. Whatever its doctrines are, they must have been ably explained and conscientiously preached by a succession of excellent men. Whatever they may have preached, according to Mr. Newman's hypothesis, it could not be truth, or it would long before this have become " popular;" so far from it, there are now but a small remnant left of true churchmen, and it has become necessary for Mr. Newman's party to recal the majority from their wandering path. If on the other hand the doctrines which they have preached *have* become popular, and *are the truth*, Mr. Newman must be in error, and must also differ from the great body of the Reformers: but his great effort is to prove the contrary. How is this inconsistency or contradiction to be explained?

Mr. Newman speaks of the Via Media,

or Anglican Church, as a system which has "never existed except on paper, and "has never been reduced to practice." It is worth inquiry, supposing this to be true, whether it has happened from the intention or neglect of the Fathers of our Church. Have they for so long a period omitted to do what Mr. Newman proposes to perform, or have they wisely left that open which he wishes to close up? He says our theory on the subject of private judgment is " neither Protestant "nor Roman, and has never been rea-"lized;" is it left for the writers of the Oxford Tracts to realize it for us according to their own fancy? Are they to determine what is the meaning of our "paper" by their "practice?" Why should not any other small party in our Church do the same? Our theory would then be realized in several different ways. Should we be better off in that case than we are now, without any positive theory at all? I humbly conceive our Reformers would have supplied this deficiency if they had supposed it to be one. I believe the fear expressed that " serious Protestants, " dissatisfied with their system, will be " take themselves to Romanism," is quite groundless, except Mr. Newman creates such a confusion between the Church of England and the Church of Rome, that many of them will be unable to distinguish the real difference.

In Mr. Newman's first lecture on the nature and ground of Protestant errors, he describes the Roman Catholic Church as depending upon one unbroken tradition from the Apostles down to the present day: that it asserts its own infallibility in such a way, as to render an appeal to antiquity wholly unnecessary. The " Mere Protestant," on the contrary, appeals to the Bible alone, and claims for himself the right of interpreting it. We are then warned of the danger of our rejecting tradition in our argument with the Romish Church, because by so doing we must eventually be compelled to reject the Bible itself, the inspiration of which can come to us by tradition only. This argument has been well termed by Dr. Shuttleworth an ingenious piece of sophistry. The history of the Bible and the interpretation of it, are widely different things. The testimony which would convince us of the one, may go a very little way in deciding us upon the other. We may surely admit upon certain evidence that a will was made by such a person, at such a time, and under such circumstances, without being compelled to take the opinions of the parties, whose evidence we are depending upon, as certain proofs of the proper construction of the will. We are surely not to be told that because the authenticity of the will, and the meaning of the testator, are supported by the same kind of evidence, that we must necessarily believe both or neither upon it; but this is exactly what Mr. Newman thinks it necessary we should do, as to the authenticity and meaning of the Scriptures. Besides which we must remember, that all the Fathers, all the Churches, and all the Councils agree in admitting the one; they perpetually differ as to the other. As we cannot, on Mr. Newman's principle, appeal to the Scriptures alone, what are we instructed to do? We are told that we must meet the Romanist upon the ground of antiquity. Now the same Church, in the same Council, at the very same time, decided in favour of the doctrine of the Trinity as we hold it in the Church of England, and against the marriage of the clergy. We know of no earlier decision upon the Trinity; Mosheim tells us that before that time private Christians were left to their own undisturbed opinions. How can we pretend to appeal to antiquity in favour of the one point, and not be bound by the same rule in the other? The whole account of the Council of Nice is, we know, very imperfect; historians cannot agree upon the time when it was held, the number of Bishops present, or what their proceedings exactly were: but all this applies to either question: the utmost which could be pretended would be, that the one decision rested on rather stronger grounds than the other. Again, what is antiquity? In 325 a Council of 318 Bishops, of whom only three belonged to the Western Church, assembled and decided upon the meaning of Scripture on the doctrine of the Trinity. In 787 another Council of 377 Bishops, of whom a very small number were of the Western Church, assembled and decreed the worship of images. In an appeal to antiquity, to *prove* the truth of either decision, all we can say is that one Council was more ancient than another, but what right have we to limit antiquity to the first 325 years of the existence of the Church? The doctrine of transubstantiation was introduced in 1215 by Innocent the Third, at a Council consisting of 412 Bishops, 800 Abbots and Priors, besides the ambassadors of almost all the European Princes. Mosheim says, " Hitherto the opinions of the ' Christian doctors, concerning the manner

" in which the body and blood of Christ
" were present in the Eucharist, were ex-
" tremely different; nor had the Church
" determined, by any clear and positive
" decree, the sentiment that was to be em-
" braced in relation to that important mat-
" ter. It was reserved for Innocent the
" Third to put an end to the liberty, which
" every Christian had hitherto enjoyed, of
" interpreting this presence in the manner
" he thought most agreeable to the decla-
" rations of Scripture." Thus the first declaration put forth with any semblance of Church authority upon this point was against us, and in favour of the Church of Rome. Where so many of the clergy were assembled, more than three times the number who met at the fourth Council at Nice, it is absurd to raise distinctions between the authority or the nature of the two Councils. The opinions of individual Fathers on this doctrine, even were they expressed much clearer than they are, can only be regarded as given in the exercise of that li-

berty which every Christian had so long enjoyed. They cannot in any way be considered as decisive of the sentiments of the Church universal. Now are we to reject this interpretation of Scripture on the authority of this Council, and then appeal to the Council of Nice to decide our dispute concerning the doctrine of the Trinity with those who differ from the interpretation which we ourselves put upon it? Mr. Newman is not satisfied with *an appeal to Scripture,* and using this early decision *as additional evidence only;* he regards it as the voice of the Church universal, which is *infallible* and *divinely secured from error;* and argues that if we reject it, we may as well reject the Scriptures themselves, as they rest on the same evidence. Let us compare the account of the Council of Nice and the decision upon the subject of the Trinity, with that just given upon Transubstantiation:—

" The subject of this fatal controversy, " which kindled such deplorable divisions

" throughout the Christian world, was the
" doctrine of three persons in the Godhead;
" a doctrine which, in the three preceding
" centuries, had happily escaped the vain
" curiosity of human researches, and been
" left undefined and undetermined by any
" particular set of ideas. The Church had
" indeed frequently decided against the
" Sabellians and others, that there was a
" real difference between the Father and
" the Son, and that the Holy Ghost was
" distinct from them both; or, as we com-
" monly speak, that three distinct persons
" exist in the Deity; but the mutual rela-
" tion of these three persons to each other,
" and the nature of the distinction that
" subsists between them, are matters that
" hitherto were neither disputed nor ex-
" plained, and with respect to which the
" Church had, consequently, observed a
" profound silence. Nothing was dictated
" to the faith of Christians in this matter,
" nor were there any modes of expression
" prescribed as requisite to be used in

" speaking of this mystery. Hence it hap-
" pened, that the Christian doctors enter-
" tained different sentiments upon this sub-
" ject without giving the least offence, and
" discoursed variously, concerning the dis-
" tinctions between Father, Son, and Holy
" Ghost; each one following his respective
" opinion with the utmost liberty."

Then arose the Arian controversy, and the Emperor Constantine assembled the famous Council of Nice in 325 to put an end to it. Mosheim goes on to say—

" In this General Council, after many
" keen debates, and violent efforts of the
" two parties, the doctrine of Arius was
" condemned; Christ declared consubstan-
" tial, or of the same essence with the Fa-
" ther; the vanquished presbyter banished
" among the Illyrians, and his followers
" compelled to give their assent to the
" creed or confession of faith, which was
" composed by this Council."

How can we possibly determine our controversy with the Romish Church by an appeal to antiquity? What inconsistency is it to compel the Socinian to bend to the decision of 325, and to refuse ourselves to yield to that of 1215! The accounts are precisely similar. It is futile to call one a Free General Council, and not the other; and equally so to say that one decision was received by the Church Universal, and the other was not so received: we are not warranted in advancing general reception in one case more than the other. Each doctrine, as Mr. Newman says of truth, made its way " by persuasion or compulsion, by " inward acceptance or by external con-" straint." Arius and his followers were allowed to choose between disgrace, banishment, or death, and acquiescing in the decision of the Council: such a decision being obtained after violent efforts on both sides. What more can be said against the freedom of the Council in 1215, or the reception of its decrees? We have no chance with the Romish Church on the ground which Mr. Newman wishes to confine us to,

We must appeal to Scripture, and assert our right to its interpretation, or we can never support *all* our points of difference with Roman Catholics. If that is the case, we cannot use one weapon against the Romish Church and another against the Protestant Dissenters; we *must* allow them the same right of appeal to, and interpretation of the Scriptures, which we claim for ourselves. At the close of this lecture Mr. Newman says, that the reformation of the Romish Church, if one awaits them, will be " far more a reform of their popular " usages and opinions, and ecclesiastical " policy, or a destruction of what is called " Popery, than of their abstract principles " and maxims." Now the " abstract prin- " ciples" are the only things worth contending about; and these are Church infallibility and the right of private judgment. What is called Popery must as inevitably follow one view of these questions, as what we have always called Protestantism does the other view of them, and if Mr. Newman deprives the Church of England of what the majority of her members consider her true principles on these points, he deprives her of every thing which a Protestant can consider valuable.

Mr. Newman's second lecture is on Romanism as neglectful of antiquity: how far he may really confute the Romish tenets, it is not my intention to inquire. I shall allude to this part of his work merely so far as to show that his arguments frequently controvert his own opinions and theory, and that his admissions in favour of the Roman Catholics, in which he is so liberal, and as I think so imprudent, must undermine the principles of the Established Church.

" In truth there is a tenet in their theo-
" logy which assumes quite a new position
" in relation to the rest, when we pass from
" the abstract and quiescent theory to the
" practical workings of the system. The
" infallibility of the Church is then found
" to be its first principle, whereas before it

" was a necessary, but a secondary doc-
" trine. Whatever principles they profess
" in theory, resembling, or coincident with
" our own, yet when they come to particu-
" lars, when they have to prove this or that
" article of their creed, they supersede the
" appeal to Scripture and antiquity by the
" pretence of the infallibility of the Church,
" thus solving the whole question by a
" summary and final interpretation both of
" antiquity and of Scripture."

Mr. Newman is so confused a thinker, or such an ambiguous and contradictory writer, that it is difficult to ascertain exactly what his real sentiments are upon the strongest and simplest points. He differs widely from what I have ever believed to be the doctrine of the Church of England, and he is quite aware that a great majority of his fellow Churchmen are of the same opinion. He appears to agree in " abstract principle" and in theory with the Romish Church on the point of Church infallibility, but differs with them upon the " practical workings of the system." He seems to admire the principle, but thinks they have made a bad use of it. Is he so blind as to conceive that infallibility in human hands can ever remain " an abstract and quiescent theory?" Can he doubt that " the practical workings " of the system" can ever be otherwise than they have been? Can he doubt that this infallibility must and will always end in " a summary and final interpretation both " of antiquity and Scripture?" Ambition in the clergy and indolence in the laity, will inevitably sooner or later bring about such consequences from such a theory. If tradition is to be an infallible guide, we are reduced in our controversy with Rome to fine-drawn and artificial distinctions upon the famous rule of Vincentius Lirinensis. We are forced to prove that, the always, everywhere, and by all, applies to our doctrines, not to theirs. Take the doctrine of the Trinity, and that of transubstantiation: can we by the assistance of this rule defend the one against the doubting ultra

Protestant, and disprove the other against the Roman Catholic? Was the decision of the Council of Nice so unanimous, its representation of the Church Universal so clear? Was the reception of its decision, enforced as it was by all the cruelties which the civil power could inflict in a barbarous age, so general? Suppose we grant that catholicity, antiquity, and consent of Fathers is not only the same *kind* of evidence of true doctrine, but the same in *degree*, as that on which we admit the authenticity of the Scriptures, the misfortune is, that the Roman Catholic Church professes to be bound by the same rule. She is not so weak as to allow, what Mr. Newman fancies he so easily proves, that it is mere *profession*. When Mr. Newman conducts the argument on both sides, he may make the ground of difference as small as he pleases; he may give up as much of principle or theory as he is inclined to do, and may finish by gaining the victory: but in the Romish communion there is far too formidable an array of talent and learning to be so trifled with. Mr. Newman may perhaps convince himself, where he would entirely fail with any candid reader. We Protestants cannot place such a reliance on his wisdom and abilities as to allow him to go out of our citadel, on the chance of his winning the battle for us there; we dare not risk our safety on such a hazardous speculation; we are afraid to grant the Roman Catholic all he would think it worth his while to ask, and trust to the chance of defeating him on " the workings of his " system." We are afraid to grant that Church infallibility is " a necessary but a secondary doctrine," and trust to the forlorn hope of proving that it ought not to be a first principle.

" Christ alone is the Author or Finisher " of our faith in all its senses; His servants " do but witness it, and their statements are " then only valuable when they are testi- " monies, not deductions or conjectures." An admission is then made, that Pope Gregory, St. Gregory Nyssen, St. Ephraim, St. Austin, St. Cyril, Tertullian, and Origen were all heterodox on the most vital points. Now in all their separate errors and heresies, do they tell us that such errors were only "deductions" and "conjectures," and not "testimonies?" They could not hold such tenets, and not suppose they were really those of the Catholic Church; if they did, they inform us that Catholicity was in their estimation no test of truth. How are we to separate deductions and conjectures from testimonies? How are we to tell when they attest and when they conjecture? *We* must not conjecture, or deduce, we must *prove*, or our pretensions to infallibility are quite groundless.

"But here it may be asked, whether it
" is possible accurately to know the limits
" of that faith, from the peculiar circum-
" stances in which it was first spread, which
" hindered it from being realized in the
" first centuries in its complete propor-
" tions."

If then the faith was not left complete

by our Saviour and the apostles, and it remained for the Church to fill up and "realize" the proportions of it, who can say when she has so filled up and realized it? Who is to decide that the great work was finished before the Council summoned by Innocent the Third? Who can positively deny, that deciding upon the doctrine of transubstantiation was a part of this task to be performed by the Church? Who can arbitrarily assert that every thing was done by the four first General Councils, and that there was nothing left for the rest to do? But we must do all this, if we are to justify our secession from the Romish Church on the grounds Mr. Newman will allow us.

The extract from Bossuet might have been found in the Oxford Tracts, and no one expression quoted from Milner could be objected to on their principles. We must surely distrust a party who make exactly the same professions. We afterwards find that Petavius, one of the most learned men who ever existed, asserts that nearly all the rulers and fathers of the Church before the Council of Nice were of the same sentiments as Arius. May not a "Mere "Protestant," upon such an authority, be allowed to *doubt* the universality or catholicity of the doctrine of the Trinity, as decided by that Council? Have we the power of condemning him for declining to rest his faith on such a decision? May he not be pardoned, if he prefers to rely on his own honest interpretation of Scripture, or the interpretation of that Church which he chooses to consult and adhere to? I shall hereafter allude to Mr. Newman's doctrine on Church authority, which is materially contradicted by his own arguments against Romanism.

We then come to the Benedictines of St. Maur, who belong to a school of Romanism distinct from the Jesuits, of whom Petavius was one. "Their learning and candour" are said to be "well known;" the following is given as a passage in their introduction to one of the works of St. Ambrose.

" It is not indeed wonderful that Ambrose should have written in this way concerning the state of souls; but what seems almost incredible is the uncertainty and inconsistency of the holy Fathers on the subject, *from the very times of the Apostles* to the Pontificate of Gregory XI and the Council of Florence, *that is for almost the whole of fourteen centuries.* For they not only differ from one another, *as ordinarily happens in such questions before the Church has defined,* but they are even inconsistent with themselves, sometimes allowing, sometimes denying to the same souls the enjoyment of the clear vision of the Divine nature."

That this instance, as Mr. Newman says, contains an acknowledgment, as far as it goes, that the religion of the Church of Rome is not that of the fathers, is true enough; but it contains something more: it contains an admission from a body of men of great candour and learning, of the uncertainty and inconsistency of the holy

Fathers, from the time of the apostles, sufficient in itself to excuse any private Christian from being *bound* by their opinions. Again we have Bellarmine, whom Bishop Marsh calls "the most acute, the "most methodical, the most comprehen-"sive, and at the same time *one of the most* "*candid*, among the controversialists of the "Church of Rome," of whom Mosheim remarks, "that his candour and plain dealing "exposed him to the censures of several "divines of his own communion; for he "collected with diligence the reasons and "objections of his adversaries, and pro-"posed them for the most part in their full "force with integrity and exactness," we have this very Bellarmine, according to Mr. Newman's own account, quoting extracts from twenty-two fathers in evidence of the Romish doctrine of purgatory, and then in recounting the errors concerning purgatory, he enumerates several of these Fathers as holding them in some of the very same passages. All this certainly causes a great destruction amongst the received Romish opinions, but what becomes of Mr. Newman's theory all this time? Are the writings of these same Fathers to be the infallible source from whence *we* are to derive *our* interpretations of Scripture, under the name of the voice of the Catholic and Universal Church? With the Scriptures so faithfully translated into our own language, are we to sacrifice our own understanding of them at such a shrine?

Again, " Medina, a Spanish Franciscan
" of the same century, well esteemed for
" his learning in the Fathers and Councils,
" when writing upon the subject of epis-
" copacy, is led to consider the opinion of
" St. Jerome, who is accused by many of
" expressing himself incorrectly concern-
" ing it." Medina's examination ended in his charging him " with agreeing with the
" Aerian heretics. Not content with this,
" he proceeds to bring a similar charge
" against Ambrose, Augustine, Ledulius,
" Primasius, Chrysostom, Theodoret, Ecu-

" menius, and Theophylact." Here is an accusation against no less than nine Fathers, by a man " well esteemed for his learning " in the fathers and the Councils," of holding heretical opinions on the subject of episcopacy. The Oxford Tracts writers deny the due reception of the Sacraments to the Scotch Church, from their want of the episcopal ordination of their clergy; this doctrine of the necessity of episcopal ordination depending, according to *their* notions, upon antiquity, which is to be gathered from the writings of these same Fathers.

" It is not surprising, with these senti-
" ments, that Romanists should have un-
" dertaken before now to suppress and cor-
" rect portions of the Fathers' writings. An
" edition of St. Austin, published at Ve-
" nice, contains the following most suspi-
" cious confession : 'Besides the recovery
" ' of many passages by collation with an-
" ' cient manuscripts, we have taken care *to*
" ' *remove whatever might infect the minds*

"'*of the faithful* with heretical pravity, or 'turn them aside from the Catholic and 'orthodox faith.'" May I ask Mr. Newman, whether we can be expected to place much reliance upon the writings of the Fathers, when they have passed through the hands of such editors? I would ask him whether, supposing any individual or any Church should be still inclined to place implicit confidence in them, they are justified in forcing such confidence upon others, by an assurance that rejecting the Fathers is the same thing as rejecting Scripture itself, because the test of truth is Catholicity, and this Catholicity, to be gathered from their writings, rests upon the same foundation as the authenticity of the Scriptures?

In the second and third lectures Mr. Newman considers the doctrine of infallibility morally and politically. He shows the moral and political consequences resulting from it, though not very clearly or perspicuously. Whenever he expresses himself strongly and plainly, it is upon questions of *practice*, not of *principle*, and the distinction he professes to draw between our Church and that of Rome is, therefore, of comparatively little consequence. I shall pass over these lectures entirely now, as I mean to quote passages from them when I come to the indefectibility of the Church.

The fifth lecture is upon the use of private judgment. " By the right of private
" judgment in matters of religious belief
" and practice, is meant the prerogative,
" considered to belong to each individual
" Christian, of ascertaining and deciding
" for himself from Scripture what is gospel
" truth, and what is not. This is the prin-
" ciple maintained in theory, as a sort of
" sacred possession or palladium, by the
" Protestantism of this day. Romanism,
" it is equally clear, takes the opposite ex-
" treme, and maintains that nothing is left
" to individual judgment; that is, that there
" is no subject in religious faith and con-
" duct on which the Church may not pro-

" nounce a decision, such as to supersede
" the private judgment, and compel the
" assent, of every one of her members. The
" English Church takes a middle course
" between these two. It considers that on
" certain definite subjects private judgment
" upon the text of Scripture has been su-
" perseded, but not by the mere authorita-
" tive sentence of the Church, but by its
" historical testimonies, delivered down
" from the Apostles' time." Now suppos-
ing the English Church has taken the extraordinary course here attributed to her, it becomes a serious question to the private Christian what " certain definite subjects" must be understood to mean. If *the Church* makes this definition, he clearly has no *right* of private judgment left. If *he* is to make it, his right of private judgment is unlimited. At this time the Church may kindly and considerately allow him a little liberty, but he is liable to lose it, as he has lost it before under the Romish Church, whenever she may choose to withdraw it

If the Church *supersedes* his private judgment, what does it matter whether it is by " its authoritative sentence" or " its histo-" rical testimony?" She is her own historian, so is not very likely to allow her testimony in that way to interfere with her decisions. She may try to soften the apparent harshness by saying this is our *testimony*, instead of this is our *sentence*, but it leaves the poor private Christian in no less a predicament on that account. I fear he would be compelled to believe the testimony, just as he would be obliged to receive the sentence; whether by " inward " persuasion," or by " external compul-" sion," depends upon how far the Church of the day is supported by the civil power in tying him to the stake, " if need be." As we have the good or evil fortune to live in an age of civil liberty, at all events we may be permitted to doubt the historical testimony of the Church, except where it agrees with Scripture itself. The Church has contradicted herself so often, and the

Anglican branch of it has notoriously dispensed with so much of her testimony, that she cannot surely *force* the reception of the rest upon any one of her members. She may assert that Church history tends to show that her own interpretation of Scripture is the same as that of the earliest ages, and thereby confirms her in such interpretation; and a great majority of her members think she can do no more.

" Now these extreme theories and their
" practical results are quite intelligible;
" whatever be their faults, want of simpli-
" city is not one of them. We see what
" they mean, how they work, what they
" result in. But the middle path adopted
" by the English Church cannot be so easily
" mastered by the mind, first because it is
" a mean, and has in consequence a com-
" plex nature, involving a combination of
" principles, and depending on multiplied
" conditions; next because it partakes of
" that indeterminateness which, as has been
" already observed, is to a certain extent a

"characteristic of English theology; lastly, because it has never been realized in any religious community, and thereby brought home to the mind through the senses. Feeling, then, the disadvantage under which the Anglican doctrine of private judgment lies, and desirous to give it something more of meaning and reality than it popularly possesses, I shall attempt to describe it first in theory, and then as if reduced to practice."

Now as to the difficulty of this middle path being mastered by the mind, I would say, that surely every man who takes orders is *expected* to understand the principles of the Church of which he is to become a Minister: whether that is always the case or not, is nothing to the purpose; the Church must expect it. She herself cannot then regard her own principles as so hard to be understood, or she never could require an infinite number of young men of every variety of intellectual capacity to comprehend them. The difficulty *may* exist in Mr. Newman's imagination: it *may* arise from an extraordinary attempt on the part of himself and his friends to wrest the principles of the Church of England so as to meet their own "peculiar" views; he may fancy he can form a Church on the joint principles of Church infallibility and the right of private judgment; but he must not attribute the difficulties he finds in his way to the Church of England. How is it with our articles, our liturgy, our Acts of Parliament, and our Church Establishment, that this middle path has never " been " realized?" How has it happened that all the learned and excellent men, who have adorned our Church since the Reformation, have allowed this indeterminateness, which has been such a characteristic of our Church, to remain a defect, if not a blemish? Why has it been left to Mr. Newman and the writers of the Oxford Tracts to realize this path, to determine these principles, and thereby supply this want? It would seem as if it must have been *designed;*

one would almost think that this long silence on the subject has been *intentional;* it is *possible* that they may have regarded this indeterminateness as the chief cornerstone in our ecclesiastical building. Mr. Newman *may,* by his anxious endeavours to remove it, bring the whole structure to the ground, leaving Roman Catholics and Dissenters to glory in its fall. The articles themselves *may* have been framed with an especial desire to embrace many persons of different shades of opinion: the very word *authority may* have been wisely chosen, to allow individual members to attach a greater or less degree of such authority to their Church, according to their judgment or inclination: it *may* have been specially intended to allow them to sacrifice their private judgment in whatever degree they may think right or proper.

Supposing this *has* been the purpose of the founders of our Church, let us consider how easy it may be for us in our day to confound their wisdom by our folly! How easy, in our mistaken attempts to perfect that which we *think* they have left imperfect, to tie up what we find has been by them left at liberty, to determine what has been by them undetermined, to "realize," in short, what they have not "realized" for us; how easy, I say, may it be for us to pull down what they have built up, to separate what they have cemented together, to destroy and bring to an end what they have with so much labour and caution erected for us.

"The internal means of judging are
" common sense, natural perception of
" right and wrong, the affections, the ima-
" gination, reason, and the like. The ex-
" ternal are such as Scripture, the existing
" Church, Tradition, Catholicity, Learning,
" Antiquity, and the National Faith. Po-
" pular Protestantism would deprive us of
" all these external means except the test
" of Holy Scripture."

Popular Protestantism *must* mean the great body of Protestants now existing in this country, including that majority of the members of our own Church who disapprove of Mr. Newman's views, and I will venture to say that this is a most unwarrantable assertion, totally unfounded in truth. A popular Protestant holds that no church has a right to *dictate* to him how far he is to be bound by the existing Church, Tradition, Catholicity, Learning, Antiquity, and the national Faith: he says that a few years ago the *then* existing Church palmed its doctrines upon him upon the especial ground of their being supported by all these assistants; is he to be told with one breath that he was then shamefully imposed upon, and with the next that he must place the same implicit confidence in the present Church? It is a libel upon the great body of Dissenters, to assert of them that they reject all these various means in their interpretation of Scripture, because they claim the right to apply them for themselves: they merely object to take all for granted upon *our*

Church, and *our* Tradition, and *our* Learning, and *our* version of Antiquity and Catholicity: they choose to go further back than the four first Councils; they choose to regard the Scripture as the oldest and most perfect history, and they will not be *forced* to admit any other; they hold that we have no authority to anathematize them on that account, supposing that they *are* wrong in their opinion: they will not allow that even if what Mr. Newman calls the Primitive Church sanctioned such a course, it became thereby just and right. What I believe to be the sentiments of our own Church on this point I shall hereafter endeavour to show.

" Most men, I say, try to dispense with
" one or other of these divine informants;
" and for this reason,—because it is diffi-
" cult to combine them; the lights they
" furnish, coming from various quarters,
" cast separate shadows, and partially in-
" tercept each other; and it is pleasanter
" to walk without doubt and without shade,

"than to have to choose which is best and
" safest."

It is curious enough to observe that the charge brought against "most men" of this day, in the beginning of Mr. Newman's volume, was their indisposition to follow the beaten and easy track which "the many, " the wise, and the good" had trodden before, and their preference of doubt and difficulty: *here* we are accused of the very opposite fault; we are blamed for a desire to walk " without doubt and without shade" rather than encounter the difficulty of choosing what is "best and safest" for ourselves. If Mr. Newman's view of the religious faults of the present generation is so changeable, we may hope that he is not very well qualified to judge what those faults really are. The meaning of "lights " casting separate shadows," if it means any thing, must be that they contradict one another; and that is the principal reason and the great justification for the " mere " protestants" rejecting the existing Church and Antiquity as *infallible* interpreters of Scripture; the light comes from so many quarters and casts so many separate shadows, that the path becomes darker from every fresh light which is admitted: as far as the existing Church and Antiquity appear to throw additional light on the study of the Scriptures, so far we are willing to make use of them, but we cannot allow that that existing Church, as her own historian, has any right to dictate to the private Christian how far he is bound to make use of such assistance; such an admission would virtually supersede the necessity or propriety of any study of the Scriptures at all.

That "the true Catholic Christian is he "who takes what God has given him, be "it greater or less; despises not the lesser "because he has received the greater, yet "puts it not before the greater, but uses "all duly to God's glory," is a truth which all Protestants would agree in; but they ask for the use of their own reason and judgment in deciding what *is* the *greater* and what the *lesser* guide.

Amongst the axioms or general rules given us for our guidance, there are two, which, taken together, will show how far the private Christian can be assisted by this publication of Mr. Newman's, either in the study of the Scriptures, or in the doctrines of the Church.

" Scripture, Antiquity, and Catholicity " cannot really contradict one another.

" When Antiquity runs counter to the " present Church in important matters we " must follow Antiquity, when in unim- " portant matters we must follow the pre- " sent Church."

We shall hereafter see that according to Mr. Newman's theory the Church is " *infallible,*" she is " *divinely secured from* " *error; what she teaches is true because* " *she teaches it,*" and all this is shown to apply to the established Church as an undoubted branch or member of the true visible Church of Christ.

We are therefore told three things —

That the present Church is certainly Catholic and follows Antiquity, and is *therefore* infallible.

That Scripture, Antiquity, and Catholicity, cannot contradict one another.

And that when Antiquity runs counter to the present Church in important matters we must follow Antiquity.

This last rule is perfectly useless, or it contains an admission that the present Church *may*, if not *does*, run counter to Antiquity, which can never contradict Catholicity; and yet in the hypothesis the present Church *is infallible because she is Catholic*, and has " authority in matters of " faith," which authority it is an abuse of private judgment to oppose or doubt.

The assertion that " it is popularly con-
" ceived that to maintain the right of pri-
" vate judgment, is to hold that no one
" has an enlightened faith who has not, as
" a point of duty, discussed the grounds
" of it and made up his mind for himself,"

is grounded in a complete misunderstanding of what the popular conception of the matter is.

If you grant the right of private judgment to Locke or Newton, you cannot deny it to the most illiterate man in the community. However desirable it might be to grant it to those only who would use and not abuse it, it cannot be done, from the absolute impossibility of drawing the line, and the want of authority in any human tribunal to attempt to draw it; the propriety, or necessity, or duty of exercising it is an entirely different question. The danger of every private Christian deducing his own creed from his own *unassisted* study of the Scriptures is only equalled by the rashness and folly of doing so, but you cannot deny him the *right*, or denounce him as a sinner for exercising it. The right cannot be granted to the age or century in which he lives and not to him. Deny the right to the age or century, and every thing is left to the clergy; Ecclesiastical History has shown us what the consequence has been; the most limited study of human nature will show us what it always must be.

"If he would possess a reverent mind, "he must begin by obeying; if he would "cherish a generous and devoted spirit, "he must begin by venturing somewhat "on uncertain information; if he would "deserve the praise of modesty and hu- "mility, he must repress his busy intellect, "and forbear to scrutinize. This is a "sufficient explanation, were there no "other, for the subscription to the Thirty- "nine Articles, which is in this place "exacted from those who come hither "for education. Were there any serious "objection to those Articles, the case "would be different." So many generous and devoted spirits have been cruelly deceived and taken advantage of by a body of men calling themselves ministers of Christ, and claiming infallibility and divine security from error, that it is no wonder the same generosity and devotion is not found in these times in the same proportion. To use Mr. Newman's own language " In truth, we have had enough, " if we would be wise," of infallible Church authority, " which, like a broken reed, " has pierced through the hand that leaned " upon it."

Without giving any opinion on the propriety of young men being called upon to signify their assent to a great number of most abstruse and difficult theological doctrines before they have had the slightest opportunity of inquiring into their truth, I may observe, that *to them* it is a mere matter of chance whether there are any serious objections or not. When our Universities were in the hands of the Roman Catholics they might have signed articles totally different; and if Mr. Newman's party succeeds they will inevitably have to do so again, and the *authorities* will not, I suppose, *then* be much more likely to admit that there are serious objections to *their* articles than we are now to *ours*. Mr. Newman's language on the occasion, is a good example of his usual assumption of the whole point at issue.

We are allowed afterwards to examine the basis of the authority of Scripture or of the Church, but not "impartially" and "candidly," which are said to mean "scep-"tically" and "arrogantly," but "with a "generous confidence in what we have "been taught; nay, not recognizing, as "will often happen, the process of inquiry "which is going on within us." How few indeed must be the number who can expect to be fortunate enough so to hit the happy medium between *examination* and *confidence* as to be able to examine, without recognizing the inquiry! It is just in the same manner in which it will appear that we are allowed to "*verify*" the Church and Tradition by Scripture: *verify* is the precise term to imply that he *may* prove them to be right, but *may not* prove them to be wrong. "In contradiction to these "expressions" (of the Romanist) "it may "surely be maintained, not only that the

" Scriptures have but one direct and un"changeable sense, but that it is such as
" in all great matters to make a forcible
" appeal to the mind, when fairly put
" before it, and to impress it with a con"viction of its being the true one."

This is Mr. Newman's answer to the assertion of the Romanist, that the Scriptures in the hands of the private Christian without an infallible interpreter, are like a nose of wax, which may be pulled either way. In the next lecture I find the following passage.

" The task proposed is such as this, —
" to determine first whether Scripture sets
" forth any dogmatic faith at all; next, if
" so, what it is; then, if it be necessary
" for salvation; then, what are its doc"trines in particular; then, what is the
" exact idea of each, which is its essence
" and its saving principle. For instance;
" a man may think he holds the doctrine
" of the Atonement, but when examined
" may be convicted of having quite mista-

"ken the meaning of the word. This
" being considered, I think it will be
" granted me by the most zealous oppo-
" nent, *that the mass of Christians are ina-*
" *dequate to such a task;* I mean, that if
" the Gospel be dogmatic, for that I am
" here assuming, if it be of the nature of
" the Articles of the Creed, or the Thirty-
" nine Articles, *the great proportion even of*
" *educated persons have not the accuracy of*
" *mind requisite for determining it.* The
" only question is, whether any accurate
" creed is necessary for the private Chris-
" tian, which orthodox Protestants always
" maintain. Consider, then, the orthodox
" Protestant doctrines, those relating to
" the Divine nature and the economy of
" Redemption, or those again arising from
" the controversy with Rome, and let me
" ask the popular religionist,—Do you
" really mean to say, that men and women
" as we find them in life are able to de-
" duce those doctrines from Scripture,
" to determine how far Scripture goes in

"implying them, the **exact weight of its** "terms, and the danger of this or that "deviation from them?

"The question is, whether Gospel *doc-* "*trine*, the special 'form of sound words' "which is called the Faith, whatever it be, "can be so ascertained."

Let any reader, educated or uneducated, contrast these passages: one is in Lecture the Fifth, on the *use* of Private Judgment, and is written against the authority of the Romish Church; the other is in Lecture the Sixth, on the abuse of Private Judgment, and is intended to support the authority of our own Church.

In one place by the same author, and in the very same book, the Scriptures are said to have but one direct and unchangeable sense, which in *all great matters* makes a forcible appeal to the mind when fairly put before it; in the other it is asserted, that "the great proportion even of educated "persons have not the accuracy of mind "requisite for determining" any of the principal doctrines of their religion from the study of the same Scriptures.

In the beginning of the sixth Lecture some hints are thrown out of allowing the right of private judgment to certain persons under certain limitations. The most advisable mode of speaking of the right of private judgment is said to be, *not* that it is the duty of all Christians, nor the right of all who are qualified, but the duty of all who are qualified. Inability to read is then stated to be a necessary obstacle to such qualification.

" But there are other impediments, less
" obvious, indeed, but quite as serious. I
" shall instance two principal ones; preju-
" dice, in the large sense of the word, whe-
" ther right or wrong prejudice, and whe-
" ther true or false in its matter;—and
" inaccuracy of mind." This is indeed
" sounding the note of promise to the ear,
" and breaking it to the hope." We may confine ourselves to one "impediment" only, "prejudice in the large sense of the

" word;" that will be found to relieve all mankind from the right or the duty of exercising their private judgment. Mr. Newman must intend that it should do so, as we were told we ought to examine with a generous confidence in our own Church, not candidly or impartially; we were to go, in short, deep enough to see that our Church was right, but not so deep as to run the risk of finding she was wrong; which means clearly enough, that we must especially take care not to divest our minds of "prejudice in the large sense of the " word."

" In the next place, let us consider what
" force prepossessions have in disqualify-
" ing us from searching Scripture dis-
" passionately for ourselves. The mass of
" men are hindered from forming their own
" views of doctrine, not only from the
" peculiar structure of the Sacred Volume,
" but from the external bias which they
" ever receive from education and other

" causes. Without proving the influence
" of prejudice, which would be superflu-
" ous, let us consider some of the effects
" of it. For instance; one man sees the
" doctrine of absolute predestination in
" Scripture so clearly, as he considers,
" that he makes it almost an article of
" saving faith; another thinks it a most
" dangerous error: one man maintains
" that the civil establishment of religion
" is commanded in Scripture, another that
" it is condemned by it. Such instances
" do not show that Scripture has no one
" certain meaning, but that it is not so
" distinct and prominent as to force itself
" upon the minds of the many against
" their various prejudices. Nor do they
" prove that all prejudice is wrong, but
" that some particular prejudices are not
" true; and that, since it is impossible to
" be without some or other, it is expedient
" to impress the mind with that which is
" true; that is, with the faith taught by

" the Catholic Church, and ascertainable
" as a matter of fact beyond the influence
" of prejudice."

I will willingly grant this existence of prejudice, the effect of it upon the admission or rejection of different theological doctrines, and the great expedience of impressing the mind " with that which is " true." But here a difficulty occurs to all Protestants now in existence, except Mr. Newman and his friends at Oxford. This is, " What *is* this truth?" Mr. Newman assumes, first, that it is " the " faith first taught by the Catholic Church," and then, that what they actually did teach is " ascertainable as a matter of fact be-" yond the influence of prejudice." If there is an existing infallible interpreter either of Scripture or of history, this truth can be obtained by application to that infallible authority, but how can it be *positively* obtained without? Mr. Newman cannot conceive that his Church, much less his very small party in it, are free from these prejudices. When accurately investigated, it turns out to be a case of the blind leading the blind, or at all events those whose vision must be very imperfect directing the steps of those whose sight is but a little more imperfect. It is a small number of prejudiced individuals, in a prejudiced Church, setting themselves up as infallible guides to their fellow-creatures in many most abstruse and difficult religious doctrines, on the plea that those fellow-creatures must themselves be under some prejudices, and therefore cannot ascertain the truth by their own reason and abilities. It is more than this; it is making the monstrous assumption that this small knot of individuals are and must be right, because antiquity is an infallible test of truth, and they can decide infallibly what *is* antiquity, and what she says, and that they are then justified in considering these fellow-creatures and fellow-wanderers as sinners and schismatics in the exact proportion in which they may differ in opinion with their self-proffered instructors.

If Antiquity *is* to decide all religious controversy, can Mr. Newman pretend that this voice of Antiquity is ascertainable as a matter of fact beyond the influence of prejudice? First, are the writings of the Fathers so clear, are they so consistent, are they so perfect, so unmutilated by the Roman Catholics, through whose hands they passed, and who have been, according to Mr. Newman's own account, so careful to amend and correct them—do we find them, I say, in such a state that even Mr. Newman and his party can ascertain the true account of what the Church Catholic really did hold during those three, four, or five centuries? In the second place, we know that this said Church Catholic was rent into fierce parties in those very centuries; that what is called the decision of the Church, was little more than the victory of one violent party over another equally violent; the reception of the decision was a matter of physical force; the vanquished minority in those ages of barbarism were banished or put to death for what were called their heretical opinions: the necessity for resorting to these measures proves how little moral respect was had for the decisions they were used to enforce. As a matter of course, the true history of the opinions of this minority has never reached us; their writings were destroyed, and we are therefore entirely in the hands of their opponents, who tell us just as much as may suit their convenience. The successful doctrine is represented as the true Catholic or Universal Faith, the unsuccessful as a new and pestilent heresy. Under all these circumstances, can we assume these two positions; first, that the Catholic faith was *necessarily* true at any particular period; and secondly, that we have an accurate account of what that faith was? Certainly not.

We have now a variety of instances

given us of different **interpretations** of Scripture. " In some places it is liberally " opened, at others it is kept close shut; " sometimes a single word is developed " into an argument, at another it is denied " to mean any thing specific or definite, " any thing but what is accidental or tran- " sient. At times the commentator is " sensitively alive to the most distant allu- " sions, at times he is impenetrable to " any; at times he decides that the sacred " text is figurative, at other times only " literal; without any assignable reason, " except that the particular religious per- " suasion to which he belongs requires " such inconsistency." Mr. Newman names several instances; as in the texts, " Do " this in remembrance of me," and " Ye " also ought to wash one another's feet;" where the Anglican Church, which is assumed to be right, interprets the Scriptures with this apparent inconsistency. The argument is, that no private Christian could possibly arrive at the orthodox interpretation of particular texts, as he could never know when to consider them literal, when figurative, &c. &c. Now the whole strength of this argument will be found to rest, as almost every other of Mr. Newman's arguments do, on the assumption, first, that the " Early Church" must be right, and secondly that the Anglican Church, as interpreted by Mr. Newman, whose interpretation is essentially different from that of a majority of her members, exactly follows that Early Church. Is it not obvious that an argument of a very opposite tendency may be grounded on these very facts? May it not reasonably be doubted from these very instances of inconsistent interpretation of Scripture, first, whether the Early Church was infallibly right, or secondly, whether we infallibly follow that Early Church? When we become so forcibly impressed with the extent of the prejudices of other sects or other men, may we not be allowed to recollect the possibility that our own Church or we ourselves *may* be in some degree under prejudices of a different kind? When we are disposed to deny that the Church of Scotland is a branch of the true Church because she does not acknowledge the necessity of Episcopal Ordination, may we not remember that all the dignities, all the wealth, and all the power which the state has conferred upon *our* Church, are to be shared or expected by us only by our adhesion to her doctrine on this and other subjects? May not this consideration of the bare possibility of such a prejudice in our minds, check our proneness to decide upon and then condemn the conduct of other Churches or other men?

Upon the various texts of Scripture, which are supposed to sanction the right of private judgment, Mr. Newman observes,

" Yet after all, can any one text be
" produced, or any comparison of texts, to
" establish the very point in hand, that
" Scripture is the sole necessary instru-

"ment of the Holy Ghost for guiding the
"individual Christian into saving truth?
"for it may be very true that we ought
"to search the Scriptures, and true that
"Scripture contains all saving doctrine,
"and true that we cannot understand it
"without the Holy Spirit, and true that
"the Holy Spirit is given to all who ask,
"and true that all perfect Christians do
"understand it, and yet there may not be
"such connection between these separate
"propositions as to make it true that men
"are led by the Holy Spirit into saving
"truth *through* the Scriptures."

Mr. Newman cannot see any medium between an infallible Church Authority, and the rejection of all instruction or assistance in the study of the Scriptures. His argument is, if you put a book into the hands of a man, telling him that it is a Bible and contains the word of God, that you *thereby* admit the authority, and absolutely make use of tradition; and that such admission must inevitably lead you to the point, that on every doctrine, or on just as many as you choose to insist upon, you are justified in compelling this man, who receives this book at your hands, to interpret it according to your directions. This is not a piece of ingenious sophistry: there is no mark of ingenuity about it. No man in his senses disputes the propriety of a parent instructing a child, the educated instructing the uneducated, the Church instructing her members. Every Dissenting body professes to *instruct*, as we do; but the great Protestant principle, that *vital* principle in which I always supposed our Church differed from that of Rome, is this, that we have no right or authority whatever for *obliging* the private Christian to be bound by our instructions or interpretation; that when we have told him what we are convinced the orthodox faith is, that we have done all we have any right to do; that we have no infallible authority to pronounce him a sinner because he cannot conscientiously accept this faith exactly as we hold it. Mr. Newman thinks differently, and therein differs from the true doctrine of the Church of England, and that of all other bodies of Protestants.

" If then one external means of infor-
" mation is admitted as intervening be-
" tween the Holy Ghost and the soul,
" though it is not mentioned, why not
" another? When Christ says, 'Seek and
" 'ye shall find,' He does not specify
" the *mode* of seeking: he means, as we
" may suppose, by all methods which are
" vouchsafed to us, and are otherwise
" specified. He includes the Church,
" which is called ' the pillar and ground
" ' of the truth.' Our service applies the
" promise to seeking God in Baptism;
" and as it may include the use of the
" sacraments, so may include the use of
" Catholic teaching."

Now what is the private Christian to do when he finds there are two Churches, holding materially different doctrines, each (according to Mr. Newman's idea of our Church) claiming Catholicity, Antiquity, and Infallibility? What is he to do if he should find himself brought up and religiously educated in the Scottish Church, which differs from both? According to Mr. Newman's theory, because he admits that one external means, the Scriptures, are to be made use of, he must make use of all; that is, he must avail himself of all this contradictory teaching: suppose he should do so, what would his religious belief be? There is however one other external means totally omitted and lost sight of by Mr. Newman, which even on his hypothesis he has as much right to use as any other: it is equally vouchsafed to him by Providence, and would appear, in the confusion which he would be in amongst these contending infallible Churches, not only to be highly useful, but absolutely necessary. This is his reason; a means which is avowedly to be his guide in all other matters, and by which alone he could comprehend what the Scriptures were. All that the " mere Protestant" asks is, that he should not be condemned by one Church because he may choose to follow the guidance of another Church: all that he requires is the free use of his reason in the choice and selection of these external means, and that he should not be made accountable to any human authority for his conduct in this respect. He claims the right to do something *more* than *verify* the doctrines of any particular Church, inasmuch as he is utterly unable to *verify* opposite doctrines from the same Scriptures: he claims the right, if he chooses to exercise it, of deciding for himself which of the doctrines proposed to him are most in accordance with Scripture. He does not claim, and has no wish whatever to exercise, the preposterous privilege of rejecting all external means in his search after truth.

In the seventh lecture, on the " In-
" stances of the abuse of private judgment,"

we have cases of erroneous opinions resulting from an appeal to Scripture, to the neglecting of tradition.

"First might be instanced many of the
"errors in matters of fact connected with
"the Scripture history, which got current
"in early times, and, being mentioned by
"this or that Father, now improperly go
"by the name of traditions, whereas they
"seem really to have originated in a mis-
"understanding of the Scripture. Such,
"for instance, is the report recorded by
"Irenæus, and coming, as he conceived,
"on good authority, that our Saviour
"lived to be forty or fifty. Such is
"Clement's statement that St. Paul was
"married; such is that of Clement and
"Justin, that our Lord was deformed in
"person. These make out no claim to
"be considered Apostolical, whereas they
"do singularly coincide generally with
"certain texts in Scripture, which admit
"of being distorted so as to countenance
"them.

"If these various opinions did really thus arise, it is a very curious circumstance that they should now be imputed to tradition, nay, and adduced, as they are popularly, as if palmary refutations of its claims, whereas they really arose from the circumstance of either going solely by Scripture, or with but scanty and insufficient guidance from tradition."

The more extensive Mr. Newman's learning and talents may be allowed to be, the more forcible will be this example how little they can protect the possessor from the most confused and inconclusive reasoning, and the most mistaken argument. The instances given profess to afford examples of the errors which may arise from following the interpretation of Scripture to the neglect of tradition. Let us take the cases separately.

First; Irenæus records, *as coming from good authority*, that our Saviour lived to be forty or fifty: Mr. Newman chooses to suppose that this mistake arose from a misinterpretation of the text, "Thou art not yet fifty years old, and hast Thou seen Abraham?" It must be a distortion of Scripture indeed to strain this into an assertion that our Saviour was then about fifty years old, or very near it. The same expression might have been used at any period of our Saviour's life. Just as we might say, What can a boy not twenty years of age know of such an event? speaking of a youth of fourteen or fifteen years old, as it might happen. In another part of Scripture, Luke iii, 23, we find that " Jesus himself began to be " about thirty years of age," and during his ministry on earth four passovers are recorded, which would make his age about thirty-four, which is what Mr. Newman considers correct, I suppose. Now this very instance is as good an example as could be afforded, how a tradition, " com-" ing on good authority," has misled a great Father in the Church, who by an attention to Scripture would have been preserved from it.

The next case is Clement's statement that St. Paul was married: this is assumed to arise from a mistaken interpretation of 1 Cor. chap. ix, ver. 5. " Have we not " power to lead about a sister, a wife, as " well as other Apostles?" St. Paul here mentions several privileges which he asserts his claim to; and at the end of the enumeration of them he says, in the 15th verse, "*But I have used none of these things.*"

Here there can surely be no room for any distortion of Scripture. The whole Scripture account shows in the plainest and simplest manner that St. Paul *was not* married; but Clement, utterly neglecting Scripture, follows a tradition in supposing that St. Paul *was* married. We may indeed see the extraordinary reasoning which can be resorted to, to favour a " peculiar development of feeling." What else can account for the inconceivable attempt to prove, from these two very cases, how dangerous it is to take the interpretation of Scripture to the neglect of tradition.

The third case proves nothing for either side of the question. The interpretation of the figurative language of prophecy, as applied to our Saviour after his existence, bears no analogy whatever to our interpretation of the Scripture in the discovery of true doctrine.

" The controversy about Baptism in
" which St. Cyprian was engaged, and in
" which, according to our own received
" opinion, he was mistaken, is a clearer
" and more important instance in point.
" Cyprian maintained that persons bap-
" tized by heretical clergy must, on being
" reconciled to the Church, be rebaptized,
" or rather that their former baptism was
" invalid. The Roman Church of the
" day held that confirmation was sufficient

"in such cases; as if that ordinance, on
"the part of the true Church, recognized
"and ratified the outward act, already
"administered by heretics, and applied
"the inward grace bound up in the Sa-
"crament, but hitherto not enjoyed by the
"parties receiving it; and she rested her
"doctrine simply on Apostolical tradition,
"which by itself might fairly be taken as
"a sufficient witness on such a point.
"Cyprian did not profess any Apostolical
"tradition on his side, but he *argued from
"Scripture* against the judgment of the
"Roman See.

"Such are the texts with which the
"African Church defended themselves in
"Cyprian's days; and who will not allow
"with great speciousness? Cyprian himself
"says in like manner, 'Usage is of no
"'force where reason is against it.' Yet,
"after all, however this may be, here is
"a case where the mere arguing from
"Scripture, without reference to tradition

" (whether voluntarily neglected or not),
" led to a conclusion which Protestants
" now will grant to be erroneous."

Before I make any remark upon this case, I will give Mosheim's account of the dispute alluded to.

" The disputes concerning the baptism
" of heretics were not carried on with that
" amicable spirit of candour, moderation,
" and impartiality, with which Dionysius
" opposed the Millenian doctrine. The
" warmth and violence that were exerted
" in this controversy were far from being
" edifying to such as were acquainted
" with the true genius of Christianity, and
" with that meekness and forbearance that
" should particularly distinguish its doc-
" tors.

" As there was no express law which
" determined the manner and form, ac-
" cording to which those who abandoned
" the heretical sects were to be received
" into the communion of the Church, the
" rules practised in this matter were not

" the same in all Christian Churches.
" Many of the Oriental and African Chris-
" tians placed recanting heretics in the
" rank of Catechumens, and admitted
" them, by baptism, into the communion
" of the faithful; whilst the greater part
" of the European Churches, considering
" the baptism of heretics as valid, used
" no other forms in their reception than
" the imposition of hands, accompanied
" with solemn prayer. This diversity pre-
" vailed for a long time without kindling
" contentions or animosities; but at length
" charity waxed cold, and the fire of ec-
" clesiastical discord broke out. In this
" century the Asiatic Christians came to
" a determination in a point that was
" hitherto, in some measure, undecided;
" and in more than one council established
" it as a law, that all heretics were to be
" baptized before their admission to the
" communion of the true Church. When
" Stephen, Bishop of Rome, was informed
" of this determination, he behaved with

" the most unchristian violence and arro-
" gance towards the Asiatic Christians,
" broke communion with them, and ex-
" cluded them from the communion of
" the Church of Rome. These haughty
" proceedings made no impression upon
" Cyprian, Bishop of Carthage, who, not-
" withstanding the menaces of the Roman
" Pontiff, assembled a council on this
" occasion, adopted, with the rest of the
" African bishops, the opinion of the
" Asiatics, and gave notice thereof to the
" imperious Stephen. The fury of the
" latter was redoubled at this notification,
" and produced many threatenings and
" invectives against Cyprian, who replied
" with great force and resolution; and in
" a second council held at Carthage, de-
" clared the baptism administered by
" heretics, void of all efficacy and
" validity: upon this the choler of
" Stephen swelled beyond measure; and
" by a decree full of invectives, which
" was received with contempt, he ex-

"communicated the African Bishops, "whose moderation on the one hand, and "the death of their imperious adversary "on the other, put an end to the violent "controversy."

Now the whole force of the argument, as the slightest examination will show, rests upon the assumption that St. Cyprian must inevitably have been in error, and that "Protestants now" must be right. An assumption, which those who Mr. Newman would call low Churchmen think we have no authority to make. Let us examine the value of this assumption according to Mr. Newman's own principles. This dispute, be it observed, is not between St. Cyprian, or even St. Cyprian and "his countrymen" on the one side, and the Romish or European Churches on the other: it was between the Asiatic and African Churches, and the European Churches. Stephen and St. Cyprian were the advocates for either party: this dispute took place about the year 252: this was about 70 years before the famous Council of Nice, and about 535 years before the last general Council held at the same place. Mr. Newman's definition of antiquity must *at least* extend to the Council in 325. By his theory the voice of the Universal Church is to decide us in preference to any interpretation we may put upon Scripture. In this Council of Nice, which is so binding upon us, out of 318 Members, there were only three of the Western Church, and amongst all the general Councils, the greatest proportion of the Western Bishops is to be found at the sixth held at Constantinople, where their number was 6 out of 56 Bishops assembled. The decisions therefore of every one of these Councils may strictly be said to be the decisions of the Eastern Church. Had a similar general Council been assembled to determine this dispute about baptism, there can be no question but that the Eastern and African Churches would have been pronounced right by that

Council:—This question only arose just before the dispute: we have no means whatever of ascertaining what the sense of the Universal Church was at any previous time upon this point. Now, one of Mr. Newman's rules is, "When an-"tiquity runs counter to the present "Church in important matters, we must "follow antiquity." This surely must be an important matter; and it would follow, not only that "Protestants now" are wrong, but that even should our Church clearly differ with St. Cyprian, we ought to follow him in preference. It is evident that such an adversary as Stephen would not be very scrupulous in quoting Tradition or any thing else in his support; but from the facts of the case, he could have no possible right to do so, as the question was never agitated till the dispute arose upon such a state of circumstances occurring.

There is another matter which deserves consideration: the great question with

Mr. Newman is, whether we ought to go by our fair interpretation of Scripture, or by antiquity. Here we have one of the most influential Bishops, so early as the year 250, supported by the Asiatic and African Churches, in at least two Councils held for the express purpose of considering and deciding upon this very question of heretic baptism; we have, I say, this Bishop, by Mr. Newman's own account, appealing to Scripture, and *against* tradition: his words are described to be, "*usage is of no force where reason is "against it.*" Now if the year 250 is included in "antiquity," and if the sense of the Catholic Church is to be taken by that of a vast majority of it (and in no other way has it ever, or can it ever be taken), there can be no doubt that we have, on Mr. Newman's own principle of being bound by this "antiquity" and the voice of the Catholic Church, a justification for following Scripture in preference to Tradition, and placing more confidence in *rea-*

on than in *usage*. Hence we see that Mr. Newman's argument for this instance of the abuse of private judgment must derive its whole force upon the ground that "Protestants now" are certainly right, when it appears plainly enough, that according to Mr. Newman's own principles they are mistaken and wrong; and in the whole case, we have on this same theory of Mr. Newman's and the Oxford Tracts writers, a positive authority for following Reason and Scripture in preference to Usage and Tradition. How far my reasoning upon the matter is fair and just, I must leave to the candid reader to judge. It is worth observing, that Stephen Bishop of Rome excommunicated St. Cyprian and all the African and Oriental Bishops and Churches; and I would ask, as Jeremy Taylor was, in the late Mr. Froude's opinion, so heretical for considering that excommunication when unjust was no evil, how far it was an evil in this case? and whether a minority in the Church (perhaps even one single bigoted and imperious individual in that minority) can be justified in inflicting such an evil on the majority on any occasion when their violent passions may prompt them to do so? If the evil is of any magnitude, it is dreadful to think we are in such hands. From the whole account of this one dispute a good lesson may be obtained upon the subject of Universal Consent, Antiquity, and the infallibility of the Church Catholic.

"Again, all members of the English
"Church at least, consider Arianism to be
"a fatal error; yet when its history is
"examined, this peculiarity will be found
"respecting it, that it appealed to Scrip-
"ture, not to Catholic Tradition. I do
"not mean to say it allowed that no one
"ever held it before its historical rise;
"but, that it did not profess, nay, it did
"not care to have the Church Universal
"on its side. It set itself against what
"was received, and owed its successes to

"the dexterity with which it argued from certain texts of the Old and New Testament. I will not enlarge on what is notorious. Arianism certainly professed in its day to be a Scriptural religion."

Supposing Arianism to have arisen from the private interpretation of Scripture, that circumstance proves merely that similar error may always arise from the same source, which no one disputes. No fair account however of this famous controversy has been handed down to us: the murder and banishment of the professors of Arian opinions, and the destruction of their writings, has left us almost, if not entirely, in the hands of their opponents, who are not quite to be depended upon. The difference in the interpretation of certain texts in Scripture might be equal, and the successful party would naturally wish to throw the weight of tradition into their scale; they would be very ready to ask, *Quis talia semper audivit?* But Mr. Newman's account is at variance with some of the best authorities, so far as they have been enabled to obtain the particulars of this controversy. Up to this period, we are informed, individual Christians held their own opinions upon the Trinity in peace and quietness. *The Church* had never given any decision upon it, and the sense of the Church cannot now be ascertained. The dispute commenced by Alexander Bishop of Alexandria, who according to Mosheim " expressed his sentiments " on this head with a high degree of free- " dom and confidence; and maintained " among other things that the Son was " not only of the same eminence and " dignity, but also of the same essence " with the Father." This doctrine was opposed by Arius, who in return promulgated *his* opinions. This word " Essence" was probably just as new to the Christian Church as any theory of the Arians could be: as the doctrine of the Trinity had so far escaped the fatal curiosity of man, any particular explication of it would be equally new, and the whole question, according to this account, arose *not* with the Arians, but with Alexander, who chose to express opinions on a subject totally beyond his comprehension with such "a "high degree of freedom and confidence." A Council was assembled at Nice, and I will just quote Dr. Jortin's account of the motives which might influence its members.

"Let us consider by what various mo-
"tives these various men might be influ-
"enced; by reverence to the Emperor, or
"to his counsellor and favourites, his slaves
"and eunuchs; by the fear of offending
"some great prelate, who had it in his
"power to insult and plague all the Bishops
"within and without his jurisdiction; by
"the dread of passing for heretics, and of
"being calumniated, reviled, hated, ana-
"thematized, excommunicated, impri-
"soned, banished, fined, beggared, starved,
"if they refused to submit; by compliance
"with some active, leading, and imperious

"spirits; by a deference to the majority;
" by a love of dictating and domineering,
" of applause and respect; by vanity and
" ambition; by a total ignorance of the
" question in debate, or a total indifference
" about it; by private friendship; by en-
" mity and resentment; by old prejudices;
" by hopes of gain; by an indolent dispo-
" sition; by good nature; by the fatigue
" of attending, and a desire to be at
" home; by the love of peace and quiet,
" and a hatred of contention, &c. &c."

Such are the various motives, which may and *must* in all human probability, have influenced many of the Bishops; then how can we depend upon their really representing the Catholic Church? The sense of the Catholic Church was very soon taken from the decisions of a few imperious Ecclesiastics, and the reception of such decision was enforced, according to Mr. Newman's expression, by " outward " compulsion," which in those days meant fire and sword. In this instance, after violent contention on both sides a majority decided against Arius, and that majority, as a matter of course, asserted theirs to be the true orthodox and ancient faith, and his to be a new heresy, which was never before heard of. The value of this example of an error arising from private interpretation of Scripture, and the neglect of Tradition, depends on the assumption that the Church had positively held the Athanasian doctrine till that period, which Ecclesiastical history is far from proving to us, and that value if obtained, amounts to a mere nothing as an argument against the right of private judgment. It by no means follows, that because Arius or his party were led into error by their private interpretation of Scripture, that the right of all mankind to exercise their understanding and reason in the investigation of the Scriptures is to be withdrawn from them.

" Another opinion, which though not an
" heresy, will be granted by the majority

"of Protestants to be an error, is the tenet
"with which the great St. Austin's name
"is commonly connected. He, as is gene-
"rally known, is among the ancient fa-
"thers the master of Predestinarianism,
"that is, of the theological opinion that
"certain persons are irreversibly ordained
"to persevere unto eternal life. He was
"engaged in controversy with the Pela-
"gians, and it is supposed, that in with-
"standing them he was hurried into the
"opposite extreme. Now it is remarkable
"that in his treatises on the subject, he
"argues from Scripture, and never appeals
"to Catholic Tradition.

"For instance, in his work on the Gift
"of Perseverance, he speaks as follows:

"'The enemy of grace presses on, and
"'urges in all ways to make it believed
"'that it is given according to our de-
"'serts, and so 'grace should no longer be
"'grace;' and are we loth to say what
"'*with the testimony of Scripture* we can
"'say? I mean, do we fear lest, if we so

"'speak, some one may be offended who cannot embrace the truth; and not rather fear lest, if we are silent, some one who is able to embrace it, may be embraced by error instead? For either Predestination is so to be preached, *as Holy Scripture plainly reveals it*, that in the predestined, the gifts and calling of God are without repentance, *or* we must confess that the grace of God is given according to our deserts, as the Pelagians consider.'

"Here it is curious indeed to see how closely he follows St. Cyprian's pattern in his mode of conducting his argument; *viz.*, a reference to certain texts of Scripture, and (if I may say it of such holy men) a venturesome, à priori, or at least abstract course of reasoning. But now let us see how he treats the objection which was made to him that his doctrine 'was contrary to the opinion of the 'Fathers and the Ecclesiastical sense.' He speaks as follows:

"'*Why should we not*, when we read in commentators of God's word, of His prescience, and of his calling of the elect, understand thereby this same Predestination? For, perhaps, they preferred the word prescience because it is more easily understood, while it does not oppose, nay, agrees with the truth which is preached concerning the Predestination of grace. Of this I am sure, that *no one could have disputed* against the Predestination, *which we maintain according to the Holy Scriptures* without an error. Yet I think those persons who ask for the opinions of commentators on this subject *ought to have been contented* with these holy men, celebrated everywhere for Christian faith and doctrine, Cyprian and Ambrose, whose clear testimonies we have given.

"' What do we seek clearer from commentators of the word of God, *if it be* "'*our pleasure to hear from them what is plain in the Scriptures.*'

"What makes the failure of this appeal to the previous belief of the Church still more remarkable, is the clear view St. Austin possesses of the value of Catholic Tradition, and the force with which he can urge it against an adversary on a proper occasion. Here then we are furnished with a serious lesson of the mischief of deducing from the sacred text against the authority of Tradition."

Assuming that the "majority of Protestants" are correct, it appears that St. Austin was led into error by following his private interpretation instead of Tradition in *this instance;* this is all that can be proved on that side, but a little is proved by this example on the other; we have the authority of St. Austin, Cyprian, and Ambrose for appealing to Scripture instead of Tradition. We are to take our interpretation from commentators only "*if it be our pleasure to hear from them what is plain in the Scriptures.*" I can easily conceive that St. Austin possessed a clear view of the value of Catholic Tradition, and could use it with great force on a "*proper occasion;*" but I have no doubt he, as well as other Fathers and most other fallible beings since their time, deemed such *proper occasions* to be when this Tradition agreed with their own opinions. Their appeal to older commentators was made as that of the Oxford Tracts writers to the Fathers in our own Church, to support their own "peculiar" views, and not otherwise.

The two remaining instances of the abuse of private judgment, are the Roman doctrine of Purgatory and that of the Pope's Universal Bishoprick. I will allow that these two errors may have arisen from this private interpretation of Scripture, and I can the more easily do so, as I would admit, if it was at all desired, that *every error* and *every heresy* which has arisen since the time of our Saviour has originated in the same source; but I would wish to make a few observations upon all these instances and the argument attempted to be drawn from them. Mr. Newman enumerates six great errors, which have *all* been the consequences, as he fancies, of exercising the right of private judgment, and he argues from this circumstance, how dangerous it must be for any individual, or any age, or any country, to trust to their interpretation of Scripture, and how much safer it is for them to adhere to Tradition. Now it signifies very little to us what Irenæus thought about our Saviour's age, or what St. Cyprian's opinion was upon Baptism; we need not inquire about Arius's doctrine upon the Trinity, or St. Austin's notion of Predestination, Augustine's doubts about Purgatory, or the Pope's tenet of his own Universal Bishoprick; if any of these errors have *done any mischief* it has been undoubtedly from the admission of the very principle which Mr. Newman and his party are so anxious to uphold and to maintain; the principle of appealing to Tradition and *not* to Scripture. Private interpretation of Scripture, whether exercised by any individual, any age, or any country, always has and ever will be liable to lead to error. But if the right of such appeal is *preserved* and *exercised*, such errors will die with the individual, the age, or the country with whom they originate. On the contrary, what are the consequences upon the principle of Tradition? What have been the consequences with the Romish Church, and must be in time with any and every Church which once admits the same principle? These errors are *handed on* and added to by one Father after another, by one age after another age, till the simple doctrines of Scripture and primitive truth become so overlaid by the continued growth of human folly and superstition, that they can scarcely be discerned amidst the rubbish by which they are surrounded. The guesses, the fancies, or the conceits of some bishop or Father about some text in Scripture, instead of terminating with his own life, become in the lapse of ages so grown and improved upon, that they are made into an important doctrine, and sanctioned and promulgated on Church authority. The very Father himself with whom the error commenced, would perhaps be infinitely more staggered with this decision of the Church Catholic, than any of the willing and superstitious parties who receive it when it is made known to them.

It is curious enough to find amongst the multitude of inconsistencies and contradictions in this volume, that no man can use the *opposite* argument better than Mr. Newman himself "*upon a proper occasion.*" In his endeavour to make out some reason for admitting the authority of the first six general councils and *not* that of the seventh, he says, "*It was the first general council which professed to ground its decrees, not on Scripture sanction, but*

"*mainly on tradition; and it was the first*
"*which framed as an article of faith what,*
"*whether true or false, was beside and*
"*beyond the articles of the Apostles'*
"*creed.*"

So evident is it, that in all human controversies, the choice of the weapons is guided by their fitness to serve the purposes of the party making use of them. Here Tradition, which would have saved St. Cyprian and St. Austin, led the whole council astray: the guide which would have saved the council lost the Fathers. Mr. Newman says, page 165, "that it may
" surely be maintained, not only that the
" Scriptures have but one direct and un-
" changeable sense, but that it is such as
" in all greater matters to make a forcible
" appeal to the mind when fairly put be-
" fore it, and to impress it with a convic-
" tion of its being the true one."

If this is true, surely we must be rash in the extreme to desert the rock of the Scriptures for the sands of Tradition: we cannot, according to Mr. Newman's own account, get far wrong by adhering to the former, even with our imperfect faculties. The necessity for Lectures on the " Errors " of Romanism," is proof enough of what evils may arise from admitting and acting upon the principle of the latter.

The eighth Lecture is upon the Indefectibility of the Catholic Church. Whatever doubt or obscurity may hang over Mr. Newman's theory in other places, we must, at all events, acquit him here in that respect. At the risk of directly contradicting his own arguments and the doctrine of the Church of England as shown in her own articles, he plainly, boldly, and unequivocally claims infallibility for the Church Catholic, and for the Anglican Church as a branch of it.

" As I have already implied, Private
" Judgment and Church Authority, in mat-
" ters of faith, do not, in principle, inter-
" fere with each other. The Church en-
" forces, on her own responsibility, what
" is an historical fact, and ascertainable

" as other facts, and obvious to the intelli-
" gence of inquirers as other facts; *viz.*,
" the doctrine of the Apostles; and pri-
" vate judgment has as little exercise here
" as in any matter of sense or experience.
" It may as well claim a right of denying
" that the Apostles existed, or that the
" Bible exists, as that that doctrine existed
" and exists. We are not free to sit at
" home and speculate about every thing;
" there are things which we look at or
" ask about if we are to know them:
" Some things are matter of opinion, others
" of inquiry. The simple question is,
" whether the Church's doctrine is Apos-
" tolic, and how far Apostolic. Now if
" we could agree in our answer from exa-
" mining Scripture, as we one and all agree
" about the general events of life, it would
" be well, but since we do not we must
" have recourse to such sources as will
" enable us to do so, if there be such; and
" such, I would contend, is Ecclesiastical
" Antiquity. There is, then, no intricacy

" and discordance of claims between the
" Church and private judgment in the ab-
" stract: the Church enforces a fact—
" Apostolical Tradition, as the doctrinal
" key to Scripture, and private judgment
" expatiates beyond the limits of that Tradi-
" tion; both the one and the other on its
" own responsibility."

We have here one of the most astonishing propositions which ever was put forth by one fallible creature to his fellow creatures. The Church enforces a fact—the doctrine of the Apostles, which is as obvious to the intelligence of inquirers as any other fact, such as the truth of Christianity or the existence of the Bible, and is therefore a mere matter of *inquiry* not of opinion. Enthusiastic attachment to some peculiar feelings or views, especially in religion, may not unnaturally be expected to carry the strongest intellect a little beyond the bounds of reason, but I could never have conceived to how great an extent this was possible till I read the passage I have quoted.

In the first place I would ask, what Mr. Newman can mean when he says, that some things are matters of opinion, others of inquiry? To come at once to the point, does he mean to assert that the truth of Christianity is not a matter of opinion? If he does, what possible object could there be in the numerous works upon the evidences of it? Why did not Paley, for instance, assert the fact simply, and leave it to the "intelligence of inquirers?" Why waste his time and talents in a laborious proof of what was not a matter of opinion? Suppose for a moment there is a distinction between matters of opinion and matters of inquiry: the individual makes the inquiry and receives the answer; is not the *truth* of that answer a matter of opinion? If not, a man's religion must entirely depend upon the accident of his first applying to a Christian, a Jew, or a Mahommedan. The answer he receives is merely an historical fact, about which he cannot doubt, as it is not a matter of opinion at all, but of inquiry merely. Now suppose the inquiry was made of a Jew and a Christian at the same moment, and two distinct and contradictory answers were received, what is to happen then: is the person making the inquiry to believe both or neither, or is he to make use of his reason (which would appear to be given to him by his Creator for this express purpose) in judging which answer was most likely to be the true one? The truth of Christianity is not a matter of opinion amongst Christians, because the fact of being or professing to be a Christian implies that the opinion is decided in favour of it. An immense body of the most enlightened nations now in existence, have admitted the evidence of the truth of Christianity to be so great and so overwhelming, that they have embraced it as their religion: in that way only can this fact be said not now to be a matter of opinion. The next question which arises is, what are the true doctrines contained in these Scriptures which we all receive and acknowledge the authenticity of? Here, according to Mr. Newman, is a matter for inquiry, not for opinion. The private Christian receives various answers from several bodies of men, each professing to be that true Church which he finds alluded to. We will, for the sake of argument, reduce the Churches to two, our own and the Church of Rome, and take one single question, that of Transubstantiation. On this point, the Anglican Church would give one answer, the Romish Church another, and I do not imagine that either would allow that her doctrine was not that of the Apostles.

Mr. Newman's argument is, that we receive the truth of Christianity upon the same *kind* of evidence as that on which we believe any one doctrine contained in the Scriptures, that they are both historical facts, and we cannot admit the one without necessarily admitting the other. He entirely forgets that the *degree* of the evidence may make some difference. The existence of Mary, Queen of Scotland, is an historical fact which, I think, no one would dispute; that she murdered her husband is another historical fact: are we thereby compelled to reject our belief in the first except we will admit the truth of the second?—but this is Mr. Newman's argument. I would submit, that the first fact is recorded in *all* histories and is believed by *all* parties; that the second is advanced in some histories and denied in others, is believed by some persons and entirely disbelieved by others. On each side the strongest assertions are made: may not an individual compare the two statements, investigate the opposing arguments, and judge of their respective truth and justice. Have either party a right to say, we merely tell you two historical facts, it is not your place to speculate on the truth of them; they are matters of inquiry, *not* of opinion, and you cannot reject the one without rejecting the other also? This case is precisely parallel to the respective claims of two Churches upon our belief in their particular interpretation of Scripture. The Romish Church asserts the doctrine of Transubstantiation, the Anglican Church denies it; just as the Romish and Anglican Churches assert the necessity of Episcopal Ordination, which the Scottish Church denies. The private Christian pleads for his right of private judgment on these points, without being compelled to give up his belief in Christianity. When Church authority confines itself to what I conceive our article does confine it, it does not interfere with private judgment; when it means the authority of a parent over a child, the old over the young, the learned over the unlearned, it may *influence* private judgment in the greatest possible degree, but does not interfere with the right of exercising it; when it *supersedes* it and *dispenses* with it, as Mr. Neuman says it does and ought to do, it must "interfere" very materially with it in principle and in practice; this must be much more "ob-"vious to the intelligence of inquirers" than any historical fact, however strongly supported or proved.

" I have said the Church's Authority in " enforcing doctrine extends only so far " as that doctrine is Apostolic, and there-" fore true; and that the evidence of this " is in kind the same as that on which we " believe the Apostles lived, laboured, and " suffered."

The inquiry is, what is really the doctrine of the Apostles, and therefore true; and if the authority of the Church extends only so far and no farther, it will never be disputed; but the private Christian cannot allow the Church to decide this question for herself. If she can, the limit proposed is ridiculous. Suppose the civil power in a despotic government is admitted to extend only to what is beneficial to the community, and the question what is and what is not beneficial is allowed to be decided by this same civil power, the sooner the restriction is taken off the better, as it cannot be of much use to the community: the civil power would soon think so too, and would take it off for herself, as the Romish Church did in the case of her authority. No true Protestant or consistent member of the Church of England would willingly give her the opportunity again. The evidence of the number of bishops who were at the Council of Nice, and of the year in which it was held, is the same in *kind* with that on which we believe that the Apostles lived, laboured, and suffered: we arrive at both facts through tradition and ecclesiastical history, but not supported by quite the same *degree* of evidence, and we therefore suppose we are bound to believe the one, and may doubt about, or disbelieve the other.

I now come to a passage which no

Protestant can read without astonishment, as coming from a professed member of a Protestant Church.

" Not only is the Church Catholic bound
" to teach the truth, but she is *ever di-*
" *vinely guided to teach it*; her witness of
" the Christian faith is a matter of promise
" as well as of duty; her discernment of
" it is secured by a heavenly as well as a
" human rule. She is indefectible in it,
" and therefore not only has authority to
" enforce, but is of authority in declaring
" it. This, it is obvious, is a much more
" imposing contemplation than any I have
" hitherto mentioned. The Church not
" only transmits the faith by human means,
" but has a supernatural gift for that pur-
" pose; that doctrine which is true, con-
" sidered as an historical fact, is true also
" *because she teaches it*. In illustration of
" this subject, I shall first consider two
" passages in our received formularies.
" First; in the 20th Article we are told
" that the Church has authority in matters

" of faith. *Now these words certainly do*
" *not merely mean that she has authority to*
" *enforce such doctrines as can historically*
" *be proved to be Apostolical.* They do
" not speak of her power of enforcing
" truth, or of her power of enforcing at
" all, but say that she has authority in
" controversies; whereas, if this authority
" depended on the mere knowledge of an
" historical fact, and much more if only
" on her persuasion in a matter of opinion,
" any individual of competent information
" has the same in his place and degree.
" The Church, then, according to this
" article, has a power which individuals
" have not; a power, not merely as the
" ruling principle of a society, to admit
" and reject members; not simply a power
" of imposing tests, but simply authority
" in matters of faith. But how can she
" have this authority unless she be cer-
" tainly true in her declarations? She
" can have no authority in declaring a lie.
" Matters of doctrine are not like matters

" of usage or custom, founded on expedi-
" ence, and determinable by discretion.
" They appeal to the conscience, and the
" conscience is subject to truth alone. It
" recognizes and follows nothing but what
" comes to it with the profession of truth.
" To say the Church has authority, and
" yet is not true, as far as it has authority,
" *were to destroy liberty of conscience*, which
" Protestantism in all its forms holds espe-
" cially sacred; it were to substitute some-
" thing besides truth as the sovereign lord
" of conscience, which would be tyranny;
" if this Protestant principle is not sur-
" rendered in the Article, which no one
" supposes it to be, the Church is there
" set forth as the organ or representative
" of truth, and its teaching is identified
" with it."

" Our reception of the Athanasian Creed
" is another proof of our holding the *in-*
" *fallibility* of the Church, as some of our
" divines express it, in matters of saving
" faith. In that Creed it is unhesitatingly

"said, that certain doctrines are neces-
"sary to be believed in order to salva-
"tion; *they are minutely and precisely
"described; no room is left for private
"judgment; none for any examination into
"Scripture, with the view of discovering
"them.*"

In the fifth lecture we find;

"One chief cause of sects among us
"is, that the Church's voice is not heard
"clearly and forcibly; *she does not exer-
"cise her own right of interpreting Scrip-
"ture; she does not arbitrate, decide, con-
"demn;* she does not answer the call
"which human nature makes upon her."

This assertion of the Infallibility of the Church is clear enough. We shall see that, according to Mr. Newman himself, there are no *degrees* of Infallibility: the qualification " as some divines express it," is as curious as it is useless. Before I make any remark upon these passages, I will first give some extracts from a previous lecture of Mr. Newman's, that the reader may judge how far they can be reconciled.

Let us go back to Lecture the Third, On the Doctrine of Infallibility morally considered. This and the following lecture is directed against the Infallibility of the Romish Church.

" Of this evil system the main tenet is " the Church's infallibility, as on the other " hand the principle of that genuine " theology out of which it has arisen is " the authority of Catholic Antiquity."

Here we have a broad distinction asserted between infallibility and authority.

" The doctrine of the Church's Infalli-" bility is made to rest upon the notion " that any degree of doubt about religious " truth is incompatible with faith, and that " an external infallible assurance is neces-" sary to exclude doubt. Proof, or cer-" tainty of the things believed, is secured " upon two conditions; if there be a God, " who cannot lie, as the source of Reve-" lation, and if the Church be Infallible

"to convey it. Otherwise it is urged,
"what is called faith is merely opinion,
"as being but partially or probably cer-
"tain. To this statement it is sufficient
"to reply here, that according to English
"principles, *faith has all it needs in having
"only the former of those two secured to
"it*, in knowing that God is our Creator
"and Preserver, and that He *may*, if it so
"happen, have spoken. This indeed is
"its trial and its praise, so to hang upon
"the thought of Him, and desire Him, as
"not to wait till it knows for certain from
"infallible informants, whether or no He
"has spoken, but to act in the way which
"seems on the whole most likely to please
"Him.

"And as well might we say, that the
"man who acts upon a letter from a
"friend does not believe his friend be-
"cause he is not infallibly sure the letter
"is not forged, as deny that such men
"have real faith as hear the Church and
"obey, *though they have no assurance that*

"*in reporting God's words she cannot err:
"*nay, doubt may even be said to be implied
"*in a Christian's* faith. Not that infallible certainty would take away all trial of our hearts and force us to obey, nor again as if nothing were clearly told us by Revelation, for much is; but *that the greater the uncertainty, the fuller exercise there is of our earnestness in seeking the truth,* and of our moral sagacity in tracing and finding it."

Here the Doctrine of Infallibility is represented as the grand distinction between the Romish Church and "English "principles." The great and proper exercise of faith is described as absolutely existing during the absence of an infallible informant.

" This leads me to notice an important
" peculiarity of Romanism, to which such
" a temper gives rise. According to its
" *theory,* the Church professes to know
" only what the Apostles knew, to have
" received just what they delivered, neither

" more nor less. But in fact she is obliged
" to pretend to a complete knowledge of
" the whole dispensation, such as the
" Apostles had not. Unless we know all
" of any subject, we must have diffi-
" culties, *and where there are difficulties,*
" *so far there is no infallible knowledge.*
" *To know some things infallibly, implies*
" *that we know all.* Or to put the mat-
" ter more clearly, where there is know-
" ledge of but a portion of a system, one
" part of what is known is more plain and
" certain than another part, and can be
" spoken of more confidently; thus the
" clearness of our view will be indefinitely
" varied, but *there are no degrees of in-*
" *fallibility.* Now partial and incomplete
" knowledge must be an inseparable at-
" tendant on a theology which reveals the
" wonders of heaven."

"Romanism, by its *pretence of Infalli-*
" *bility*, lowers the standard and quality
" of Gospel obedience, as well as impairs

"its mysterious and sacred character, and this in various ways."

"In the former Lectures it was observed, that the abstract and professed principles of both systems were often the same; but that in practice, *the question of the Church's Infallibility created a wide and serious difference between them.*"

In Lecture the Fourth, on Infallibility politically considered, we find,—

"We, for our part, have been taught to consider that faith in its degree as well as conduct, must be guided by probabilities, and that doubt is ever our portion in this life."

"We can bear to confess that other systems have their unanswerable arguments in matters of detail, *and that we are but striking a balance between difficulties on both sides; that we are following as the voice of God what on the whole we have reason to think such.*"

"Those who are thus minded, will be

"patient under the inconveniences of an
"historical controversy. Perceiving that
"on the whole facts point to certain defi-
"nite conclusions, and not to their con-
"traries, they will act upon those conclu-
"sions unhesitatingly; illuminate what,
"though true, is obscure, by acting upon
"it; *call upon others to do the same, and
"leave them to God if they will refuse.*"

"It is quite fair, indeed, or rather a
"duty to deduce truths from Scripture for
"ourselves, when we have no other guide;
"but to *enforce such deductions upon
"others is plainly unjustifiable.*"

In the fifth lecture, on the Use of Private Judgment, we read,—

"I consider then, on the whole, that
"however difficult it may be in theory to
"determine when we must go by our own
"view of Scripture, and when by the
"decision of the Church, yet in practice
"there would be little or no difficulty at
"all. *Without claiming infallibility, the*

"*Church may claim the confidence and obedience of her members.*"

In the eighth lecture we read,

"They ask triumphantly, which is the one true and infallible Church? implying, that if Scripture names but one, it must be theirs; but we may answer, *that since the Church is now not one, it is not infallible;* since the *one* has become in one sense many, the full prophetical idea is not now fulfilled; and, with the idea, is lost the full description, *and the attribute of Infallibility in particular, supposing that were ever included in it.*

"This then is the conclusion we arrive at; that the Church Catholic, being no longer one in the fullest sense, does not enjoy her predicted privileges in the fullest sense. *And that purity of doctrine* is one of the privileges thus infringed, is plain from the simple fact, that the separate branches of the Church do disagree with each other in the de-

"tails of faith; discordance among wit-
"nesses of the truth, which once was not,
"being the visible proof of its being
"impaired, as well as the sacramental
"cause of it.

"Thus both Protestantism and Roman-
"ism hold the existence of an authorita-
"tive judge of the sense of Scripture,
"*whereas our Article preserves a signifi-
"cant silence about it.*"

Let any candid person compare these passages with those in which our reception of the Athanasian Creed is said to be a proof of our holding the *infallibility* of the Church; or where the Church is said to be " divinely guided to teach" the truth, and that " her discernment of it is "secured by a heavenly rule," where she is said to transmit the faith not only by human means, but has a " supernatural "gift for that purpose;" and that doctrine, which is true considered as an historical fact, "*is true also because she teaches* "*it.*" Whoever undertakes to review a book as I have attempted to do this of Mr. Newman's, must lay himself open to the charge of giving garbled extracts and unfair representations: he cannot transcribe the whole work, so is compelled to make extracts from it. All I can say to such a charge, if made against myself, is, I appeal to the book itself: the reader must judge how far the accusation may be just. Attempts are made to draw distinctions between Infallible altogether, and Infallible "*in matters of saving faith*" only. But our author tells us, and tells us truly, that there can be no *degrees* in infallibility: if we pretend to know some points *infallibly*, our knowing *all* must be implied. Again, the Church is said to be infallible, not as a judge but as a witness; "the " Church enforces on her own responsi-" bility what is an historical fact, *viz.* the " doctrine of the Apostles." But again it is said in the very next page, " that these " words (authority in controversies of faith) " *certainly do not merely mean that she has* "*authority to enforce such doctrines as can be historically proved to be Apostolical.*" How is it *possible* to reconcile all this? I wish to confute every syllable that Mr. Newman advances in favour of the infallibility of the Church, and against the right of private judgment. On those two points he goes as far as *any* Papist can: the only difference he makes between the Romish and Anglican Churches is, that *just now* the latter is rather more mild in the exercise of this infallible authority than the former. How long that moderation may last, depends entirely on herself; she has only to extend her enumeration of " matters of saving faith." But on the other hand I can scarcely express myself better or more forcibly against these very positions, than Mr. Newman himself does, when arguing against the Romish doctrine of infallibility. He goes as far there as any " mere Protestant " need desire, because I would remind him that there can be no *degrees* in the right

H

of Private Judgment. If the Church grants it on one point, she *must* grant it on all. She may warn, or persuade, or influence; she may have *authority*, but she cannot anathematize. The restraining the matter to doctrines of " saving faith," is a mere quibble if the Church is to determine what and how many those doctrines are.

There may be infinitely greater risk in the rejection of one doctrine than of another doctrine; one article of our belief may be much more important than another article; one may be absolutely necessary to our salvation, and another may *not* be absolutely necessary; the possibility of the Church being mistaken in one doctrine may scarcely be conceivable; she may very probably be in error upon another doctrine; but she cannot, according to Mr. Newman's own showing, be *infallible* in one point, and *not be infallible* in all points. If you deny the right of Private Judgment upon one point, you certainly cannot grant it upon any. Nor can you grant this right to one individual and deny it to another, on account of any supposed capacity or fitness to judge in the one instance, and incapacity or unfitness in another instance; because how is the line of distinction to be drawn, or who is to draw it? The learned and the unlearned, the wise and the ignorant, must stand on the same footing as far as this *right* of judging for themselves is concerned, though the uncontrolled exercise of it may be infinitely more rash and hazardous in the one case than in the other. There can be no *via media* between the right of Private Judgment and Church Infallibility.

Mr. Newman argues that we attribute " Authority" to the Church in our 20th Article; and as she can have no authority in declaring a lie, she *must* be true; and to think or assert otherwise is to destroy liberty of conscience, which on this occasion Mr. Newman appears to put a high value upon. I never remember reading any parallel to this reasoning. There have been many advocates for Church Infallibility and as many for liberty of conscience, but it is truly astonishing to find it advanced that we must grant Church Infallibility for fear of destroying liberty of conscience. It has hitherto been taken for granted that the two principles were totally incompatible, whichever might be the true one. But what necessary connection is there between Authority and infallible truth? We may speak of the Authority of a Church, the Authority of a book, or the Authority of a parent, meaning thereby the *very high degree of probability which there is* that we shall therein find the truth; and it is certainly true that there can be no authority vested in any quarter " to declare ,, a lie:" but how can it be deduced from those two positions, that the answer we receive from any such authority *must* be true, or that we, by attributing authority to a Church, thereby admit that she must be infallible?

I will now attempt to show how far Mr. Newman is justified in the arguments and expressions he makes use of, by those very articles to which he appeals.

The sixth article says,

" Holy Scripture containeth all things
" necessary to salvation; so that whatso-
" ever is not read therein, nor may be
" proved thereby, is not to be required of
" any man that it should be believed as an
" article of faith, or to be thought requisite
" or necessary to salvation."

In Burnet's exposition of this article (and his work is one of pretty good authority in our Church), he observes,

" We on the contrary affirm, that the
" Scriptures are a complete Rule of Faith,
" and that the whole Christian religion is
" contained in them and nowhere else;
" and although we make great use of tra-
" dition, especially that which is most an-
" cient and nearest the source, to help us
" to a clear understanding of the Scrip-
" tures; yet as to matters of faith we reject

" all oral tradition, as an incompetent mean
" of conveying down doctrines to us, and
" we refuse to receive any doctrine, that is
" not either expressly contained in Scrip-
" ture, or clearly proved from it.

" The great objection to this is, that the
" Scriptures are dark, that the same place
" is capable of different senses, the literal
" and the mystical; and therefore, since we
" cannot understand the true sense of Scrip-
" ture, we must not argue from it, but seek
" for an interpreter of it on whom we may
" depend.

" In answer to this, it is to be considered
" that the Old Testament was delivered to
" the whole nation of the Jews; that Moses
" was read in the synagogue, in the hear-
" ing of the women and children; that the
" whole nation was to take their doctrine
" and rules from it; all appeal was made
" to the law and the prophets among them;
" and though the prophecies of the Old
" Testament were, in their style and whole
" contexture, dark, and hard to be under-

" stood, yet when so great a question as
" this, 'Who was the true Messias?' came
" to be examined, the proofs urged for it,
" were passages in the Old Testament.
" Now the question was, how these were
" to be understood? *No appeal was here
" made to tradition, or to Church authority,
" but only by the enemies of our Saviour.*

" Whereas He and his disciples urge
" these passages in their true sense, and in
" the consequences that arose from them.
" They did in that appeal to the rational
" faculties of those to whom they spoke.
" The Christian religion was at first deli-
" vered to poor and simple multitudes, who
" were both illiterate and weak; the Epis-
" tles, which are by much the hardest to be
" understood of the whole New Testament,
" were addressed to the whole Churches,
" to all the faithful or saints; that is, to
" all Christians in those Churches. These
" were afterwards read in all their assem-
" blies. Upon this it may be reasonably
" asked, were these writings clear in that

" age or were they not? If they were not,
" it is unaccountable why they were ad-
" dressed to the whole body, and how they
" came to be received and entertained as
" they were. It is the end of speech and
" writing to make things to be understood,
" and it is not supposable, that men in-
" spired by the Holy Ghost either could
" not or would not express themselves so
" as they should be clearly understood."

Now the New Dispensation, he goes on to say, is opposed to the Old as light is to darkness, and if there was no need of a certain expounder of Scripture then, there is much less now. "*Nor is there any pro-*
"*vision made in the New for a sure guide;*" from which we may conclude that the books of the New Testament were clear in those days, and they are so now, and we "*may*
"*well understand all that is necessary to*
"*salvation in the Scripture.*"

When the article speaks of the necessity of proving every thing necessary to salvation by Scripture, what can it mean?

There can be no use in the Church *proving* the doctrines she professes to teach, except the proof is to be submitted to the reasoning faculties of her hearers. But if the fact of her teaching them is of itself the proof of their truth, as Mr. Newman asserts, this second proof is totally unnecessary: the article could never have declared that the doctrines were to be *proved*, if that was implied in their being *taught*. Observe the expression is *proving*, not *verifying*, which latter word is invented to reconcile infallible authority with the right of private judgment: its signification is, that we should be allowed to prove that the doctrines taught are true, but not to discover that they can be false.

In Burnet's exposition of the 18th article, he says,

" As to such to whom the Christian re-
" ligion is revealed, there can be no ques-
" tion made, for it is certain they are un-
" der an indispensable obligation to obey
" and follow that which is so graciously

"revealed to them: *they are bound to fol-*
"low it according to what they are in their
"consciences persuaded is its true sense and
"meaning."

Burnet's idea of liberty of conscience does not appear much to resemble Mr. Newman's notion of it.

In the 19th article we read,

"As the Church of Jerusalem, Alexan-
"dria, and Antioch have erred, so also the
"Church of Rome hath erred, not only in
"their living and manner of ceremonies,
"but also in matters of faith."

How can these plain and express words be made to agree with Mr. Newman's assertion that "the Church is ever divinely "guided to teach the truth"—that what she teaches is "true *because* she teaches it?" How can we, who admit such an article, be said to "hold the *infallibility*" of the Church? The Church of England can surely claim no divine security from error, which the Churches of Jerusalem, Alexandria, and Antioch were denied. Suppose, for the sake of argument, that this infallibility is said to rest with all these Churches collectively, and not individually, or to some certain date and not afterwards, who is to assure us *infallibly* what their collective interpretation is, or was previous to that date?

On this article Burnet says,

"This article, together with some that follow it, relates to the fundamental difference between us and the Church of Rome. *They teaching that we are to judge of doctrines by the authority and decisions of the Church, whereas we affirm, that we are first to examine the doctrine, and according to that, judge of the purity of the Church.*"

There is a good deal of discrepancy between Burnet's and Mr. Newman's account of the doctrine of the Anglican Church. We cannot argue in a circle: we undoubtedly cannot find out a true Church by the purity of her doctrines, and then receive these same doctrines as pure *because she teaches them.*

I cannot quote Burnet's whole exposition of this article, and as almost every syllable of it appears to me so *directly contrary* to Mr. Newman's opinions, that I am unable to make any selection of passages from it, I would entreat the reader to compare them together.

On the authority of the Church in matters of faith, Burnet says,

" Here a distinction is to be made be-
" tween an authority that is absolute, and
" founded on infallibility; and an autho-
" rity of order. The former is very for-
" mally disclaimed by our Church, but the
" second may be well maintained, though
" we assert no unerring authority. *Every*
" *single man has a right to search the Scrip-*
" *tures and to take his faith from them;*
" yet it is certain that he may be mistaken
" in it.

" When any synod of the clergy has so
" far examined a point, as to settle their
" opinions about it, they may certainly de-
" cree that such is their doctrine; and as

" they judge it to be more or less import-
" ant, they may either restrain any other
" opinion, or may require positive declara-
" tions about it, either of all in their com-
" munion, or at least of all whom they ad-
" mit to minister in holy things.

" This is only an authority of order, for
" the maintenance of union and edification;
" *and in this a body does no more as it is*
" *a body, than what every single individual*
" *has a right to do for himself.* He exa-
" mines a doctrine that is laid before him,
" he forms his own opinion upon it, and
" pursuant to that he must judge with whom
" he can hold communion, and from whom
" he must separate. When such definitions
" are made by the body of pastors in any
" Church, all persons within that Church
" do owe great respect to their decisions.
" Every man that finds his own thoughts
" differ from them, ought to examine the
" matter over again, with much attention
" and care, freeing himself all he can from
" prejudice and obstinacy; with a just dis-

" trust of his own understanding, and an
" humble respect to the judgment of his
" superiors. This is due to the considera-
" tions of peace and union, and to that
" authority which the Church has to main-
" tain it. But if, after all possible methods
" of inquiry, a man cannot master his
" thoughts, or make them agree with the
" public decisions, his conscience is *not
" under bonds; since this authority is not
" absolute, or grounded on a promise of in-
" fallibility.*

" This is a tenet that, with relation to
" National Churches and their decisions,
" is held by the Church of Rome as well
" as by us. For they place infallibility
" either in the Pope, or in the Universal
" Church. *But no man ever dreamt of in-
" fallibility in a particular or National
" Church:* and the point in this *article is
" only concerning particular Churches;* for
" the head of General Councils comes in
" upon the next."

It must be evident that either Burnet or

Mr. Newman must be entirely mistaken in their construction of this article, as they understand the word authority in quite a different sense. In Burnet's sense, an authority may be attributed to any extent to our Church, without ever in the slightest degree interfering with the right of private judgment. If, on the other hand, it is to be understood as Mr. Newman explains it, the right of private judgment exists but in sound; it is a mere phantom of the imagination, and the sooner it is forgotten the better.

Burnet goes on,

"The Church's being called a witness of
" Holy Writ, is not to be resolved into any
" judgment that they pass upon it, as a
" body of men that have authority to judge
" and give sentence, so that the canonical-
" ness or the uncanonicalness of any book
" shall depend upon their testimony.

" The Church of Rome is guilty of a
" manifest circle in this matter; for they
" say they believe the Scriptures upon the

" authority of the Church, and they do
" again believe the authority of the Church,
" because of the testimony of the Scrip-
" ture concerning it."

" This is as false reasoning as can be
" imagined. For nothing can be proved
" by another authority, till that authority is
" first fixt and proved." And this he truly exemplifies and proves.

Let us now consider the authority of General Councils, the only mode in which it can be pretended that the sense of the Church Universal can be made known or determined.

The article is,

" General Councils may not be gathered
" together without the commandment and
" will of Princes. And when they be ga-
" thered together (forasmuch as they be an
" assembly of men, whereof all be not go-
" verned with the Spirit of God) they may
" err, and sometimes have erred, even in
" things pertaining to God. Wherefore
" things ordained by them as necessary to

" salvation, have neither strength nor au-
" thority, unless it may be declared that
" they are taken out of Holy Scriptures."

Burnet thus explains this article:—

" There are two particulars settled in
" this article. The one is the power of
" calling of Councils, at least an assertion
" that they cannot be called without the
" will of Princes. The other is the autho-
" rity of General Councils, *that they are*
" *not infallible*, and that some have erred;
" and therefore the inference is justly made,
" *that whatever authority they may have in*
" *the rule and government of the Church,*
" their decision in matters necessary to sal-
" vation ought to be examined by the word
" of God, and are not to be submitted to,
" unless it appears that they are conform
" to the Scripture."

The whole authority of the decision of any General Council, is here explicitly said to depend upon its being *conform* to Scripture. It must bear examination, and by whom? Obviously not by the Council itself, but by the age, the country, or the individual, who is expected to receive the decision with deference and respect. The sense of the Catholic Church in the early ages, or the voice of " Primitive Antiquity," as Mr. Newman might call it, and to which he professes such unlimited submission, can only be ascertained, if it is possible to ascertain it at all, by the decisions of the General Councils in those ages. Now if a doctrine is true *because* the Church teaches, or has taught it, and the teaching of the Church is only known through and by means of the decisions of General Councils, it follows that the decisions of such General Councils upon any points of doctrine, are true *because* they are so given or made: this theory is, I think, considerably at variance with the 21st article, and Burnet's explanation of it. The examination of these decisions by Scripture must be entirely a work of supererogation, if their truth is inevitable, and necessarily implied in them. We cannot first prove the decisions by an appeal to the Scriptures, and then accept an interpretation of the same Scriptures on the authority of the decisions. Both Burnet and Tomline, whose exposition of the Thirty-nine Articles are put into the hands of all candidates for orders, give an interpretation of them directly contrary to Mr. Newman's opinions. Tomline says, on this point, touching the authority of Councils,

" We reverence the Councils for the sake
" of the doctrines which they declared and
" maintained, but we do not believe the
" doctrines upon the authority of the
" Councils."

Mr. Newman asserts, that " our reception
" of the Athanasian Creed is another proof
" of our holding the infallibility of the
" Church. In that Creed it is unhesitat-
" ingly said, that certain doctrines are ne-
" cessary to salvation; they are minutely
" and precisely described; no room is left
" for private judgment; none for examina-
" tion into Scripture, with the view of
" discovering them."

Bishop Tomline truly said that "it is "certainly to be lamented, that assertions "of so peremptory a nature, unexplained, "and unqualified, should have been used "in any human composition." And he afterwards most reasonably argues, that our Church would have judged well to have rejected the damnatory clauses. The great vindication for the English Church against the charge of uncharitableness, in having allowed them to remain, has always been that she retained them with certain limitations, and that it is hard upon her to deny her the right to shelter herself under such explanation. This vindication, *which is the only possible justification the Anglican Church* (as distinguished from the Romish Church) can plead, is quite repudiated by Mr. Newman; he understands the clauses in the most obnoxious and uncharitable sense; but he must not be allowed, by his bare assertion, to fasten this interpretation upon the Church of England: here, as in other instances, he is entirely at variance with her. There are two great points to be attended to in connection with this creed: *viz.* the damnatory clauses, and the explication of the Trinity: they are totally distinct, however those clauses may be, or ought to be applied. The explication of the doctrine of the Trinity may be correct according to Scripture, but yet the Church may not be justified in denouncing eternal damnation against all those who do not admit such explication: she cannot be justified in such denouncement, except upon the certainty, first that she *must* be infallibly right in this explication, and then that a belief in such explication *must* be necessary for salvation, and we have no authority whatever for *deciding* either of those propositions in the affirmative. The Church of England does not pretend to do so. I will here give a quotation from Mr. Hartwell Horne's defence of the Athanasian Creed, he is admitted to be one of the most able and candid collectors of authorities now living.

"We now come to the fourth objection, which charges our National Church and her members with being guilty of great uncharitableness in consigning to eternal perdition all who do not assent to, or believe, every clause or verse of the Athanasian Creed. *God forbid that this should be the meaning of any creed, or of any advocate for it.* For it is to be observed, that the condemning, or damnatory clauses, as they have been called, *do not extend to each of the explications* given in the Athanasian Creed, but are intended only to secure the general doctrine. It is not the reception of the *form of words* used in this creed, but the belief of the Catholic or universal faith, which is represented as necessary to salvation; nor is it the objecting to the mode of expression here employed, *but the wilful and deliberate corruption of the Catholic faith*, which is asserted to expose a man to the danger of condemnation.

"All, therefore, that is required of us, in

" the Athanasian Creed, as necessary to sal-
" vation, is, that before all things we hold the
" Catholic faith; which faith, it is said in the
" second verse, which faith, received from
" the beginning, and to be preserved to the
" end, as embraced by the Universal Church,
" except every one do keep whole (without
" rejecting any part of it that is clearly re-
" vealed) and undefiled (without adding
" any thing to it, which may defeat its
" sense and corrupt its tendency) without
" doubt (that is, it is beyond all contro-
" versy if the Scriptures be true) he shall
" perish everlastingly (he will finally for-
" feit his title to the benefit of the Christian
" covenant). In the third and fourth verses
" the Catholic faith is stated to be this,
" that we worship one God in Trinity and
" Trinity in Unity, neither confounding the
" persons (as the ancient Sabellians and
" others did, and as some in our own coun-
" try do at this day), nor dividing the sub-
" stance, as the Arians did and do.

" This, it is declared, is necessary to be

" believed; but all that follows, from the
" fifth to the twenty-fifth verse inclusive,
" is only brought as a proof and illustra-
" tion of it, and therefore requires our as-
" sent no more than a sermon does, which
" is written in order to prove or illustrate
" a text. The text is confessedly the word
" of God, and therefore is necessarily to be
" believed; but no person is for that reason
" bound to believe every particular of the
" sermon deduced from it, upon pain of
" damnation, even though every tittle of it
" be true."

Amongst the multitude of authorities which might be quoted, supporting this view of the Athanasian Creed, as used and adopted by our Church, I will only add one, the late Dr. E. Burton, a name which is a host in itself. In his sermons, preached before the University of Oxford, he remarks on this creed—

" I wish it could be added, that the
" members of our own Church do not some-
" times follow the example which they con-

" demn; and that some among us might
" not be found to resemble the Churches of
" Rome or of Calvin, in restricting salva-
" tion to themselves, and in excluding those
" who differ from them. It being my in-
" tention to defend what is commonly called
" the Athanasian Creed, I have thought it
" right to make these remarks, and so far
" to clear the ground as to separate myself
" from those who would go *beyond* the let-
" ter of Scripture in limiting salvation, and
" to express my disapproval of those who
" presumptuously and uncharitably pass
" sentence upon all who differ from them.
" Thus, while I undertake to prove that
" our Church has adopted no confession of
" faith which cannot be supported by Scrip-
" ture, I see not that our Church directs us
" to pronounce those persons excluded from
" salvation who reject any of her confes-
" sions. We may think our own opinions
" right, and we may bless God, who has
" placed us in the way which leadeth unto
" life: *but who art thou that judgest an-*

"*other man's servant? To his own master*
"*he standeth or falleth.* It is perhaps im-
"possible, with our present feelings and
"imperfections, not to think other persons
"in error: but there is nothing which
"compels us to ascribe this errror to the
"heart: and our own condition is one of
"fearful apprehension, if we persuade our-
"selves that God will not pardon even
"errors of the heart.

"It will perhaps be said, that there are
"two declarations in the Athanasian Creed,
"which are at variance with the remarks
"which have now been made. I allude
"to what are commonly called the damna-
"tory clauses at the beginning and the end
"of the Creed. It begins with saying,
"'Whosoever will be saved, before all
"'things it is necessary that he hold the
"'Catholic faith; which faith, except every
"'one do keep whole and undefiled, with-
"'out doubt he will perish everlastingly;'
"and at the end we read, 'This is the Ca-
"'tholic faith, which except a man believe

" 'faithfully he cannot be saved.' The
" person who makes these declarations ap-
" pears undoubtedly to give an opinion
" not only as to his own, but as to others'
" salvation; and some persons who believe
" implicitly the doctrines contained in the
" creed, are unwilling to speak thus strongly
" and severely of those who do not believe
" them. *I would certainly make a broad
" distinction between the doctrines themselves,
" and this general declaration concerning
" the reception or denial of them. The two
" things are essentially different and uncon-
" nected;* or at least the doctrines may be
" true, and our own salvation may depend
" upon our belief of them, and yet it may
" not be necessary or even proper for us to
" say of another person, 'that without doubt
" 'he will perish everlastingly.' If the
" question should be raised, whether these
" clauses should be retained, and read pub-
" licly in our Churches, we might perhaps
" be led by Christian humility and Chris-
" tian charity, to wish for their removal;

" but this is a very different thing from our
" saying and believing of the doctrines
" contained in the creed, This is the
" Catholic faith."

The truth is, we do not adopt the damnatory clauses in the bigotted and uncharitable sense which they would naturally imply, and in which they were originally written. They were composed at a time when we read "of one body of Christians anathe-
" matizing another for what appears, even
" to good and pious minds, a mere verbal
" distinction:" when we see " Council after
" Council, and Creed after Creed, contract-
" ing instead of extending the limits of the
" Church, and cannot in fairness perceive
" any difference in the spirit of the con-
" tending parties, nor can we say that
" Christian charity tempered the fervour
" of Christian zeal on one side more than
" on the other."

" Well may we *blush*," to use the words of the same author, "*for the rancour of polemical warfare, particularly in the* "*fourth century*," that time which, under the name of "Primitive Antiquity," is to *supersede* and *dispense* with our reason in the interpretation of the Scriptures.

In the same sermons I meet with a definition of liberty of conscience, not very similar to Mr. Newman's idea of it, and quite incompatible with the Church infallibility which he advocates.

" We may often hear it said, that every
" man has a right to serve God according
" to his conscience: and in a certain sense
" the words are true. If it be meant that
" *every man's own conscience must judge of*
" *the revealed will of God, and that no man*
" *should be called upon to believe what, ac-*
" *cording to his own judgment, is not con-*
" *tained in the Scriptures, then we may as-*
" *sent to the proposition—that every man*
" *has a right to serve God according to his*
" *conscience*."

The commissioners, who were appointed to review and correct the Liturgy in 1689, prepared a rubric appointing on what days the Athanasian Creed should be read, which rubric concludes thus:—

" The articles of which (the Athanasian Creed) ought to be received and believed as being agreeable to the Holy Scriptures. *And the condemning clauses are to be understood as relating only to those, who obstinately deny the substance of the Christian faith.*"

I hope an immense majority of the members of our Church, lay and clerical, would be sorry to suppose that Mr. Newman's interpretation of the damnatory clauses in the Athanasian Creed was not "peculiar" to himself and a very small "remnant."

The proof of our "holding the infallibility of the Church," cannot be drawn from our adoption of this Creed, except upon the understanding that the doctrines in it are "minutely and precisely described," that these clauses apply to that minute and precise description, *and that the Church takes upon herself to make such an application of them.* The latter is necessarily implied by Mr. Newman's argument. It may be worth while to inquire shortly how far so uncharitable a denunciation can be *verified* by Scripture. The foundation for all anathemas pronounced by the Church, must be found in the 16th verse of the 16th chapter of St. Mark's Gospel, where we read, "He that believeth and is baptized "shall be saved; but he that believeth "not shall be damned." Mr. Newman's reasoning upon this text would be, he that believeth not the Gospel shall be damned, the doctrine of the Trinity is contained in the Gospel, the Athanasian Creed contains a "*minute and precise description*" of that doctrine, and *therefore* whoever rejects such minute and precise description shall be damned. We will suppose the sentence pronounced by the Church to be declaratory, not judicial; but even then all the Church can be justified in doing (except she be an infallible interpreter) is to *declare* our Saviour's sentence: she can have no right to add to it, or enlarge it, and enforce such addition and enlargement as from authority. Where erroneous doctrines or explanations of doctrines arise, the Church may be warranted, nay, called upon, to counteract, by her teaching, these erroneous explanations: she may put forth what her own impression is upon any doctrine, but she cannot attach the same penalty to the rejection of the forms of expression she may think proper to use as to the rejection of the Gospel itself: without her infallibility is granted, her explanation may *possibly* be mistaken. Again, the mistaken apprehension of so mysterious a doctrine as that of the Trinity, *may* not be the same error, or bring the same consequences upon the individual, as the disbelief of Scripture itself. When we find the declaration, " Jesus Christ is the Son " of God," we may assert on the authority of the verse in St. Mark, that whosoever denies that fact or doctrine shall forfeit his salvation ; that is, lose the pardon which is promised on condition of belief in the

Scriptures. But how can we be justified in explaining this expression, "Son of "God," by any human reasoning or analogy, however clear and unexceptionable it may appear, and then enforcing such explanation, such new forms of expression, upon the consciences of all Christians under pain of everlasting damnation? The terms "substance" and "essence" may, or may not be beneficially used to prevent or contradict a false apprehension of the doctrine of the Trinity, but where can we find any justification in Scripture for *necessarily* connecting belief in such terms or expressions with the obtaining or forfeiting salvation? If the Church could, by its own authority, make the reception of the famous word ομοουσιος *necessary*, where was that authority to stop? Who can assign any limits to it? The Church of Rome, consistently enough, assumes infallibility, and makes belief in any or all the explanations of doctrines she chooses to give necessary to salvation; and *we*

cannot admit the word ομοουσιος as a necessary article of belief on Church authority, and reject any thing else the Church may have decided upon. She had just as much right to decide upon Transubstantiation, as upon this word ομοουσιος, as far as her authority is concerned. If there is an appeal to Scripture, which Mr. Newman denies, we can be allowed to think she has proved her decision scriptural in one case and not in the other, and on no other grounds can we be justified in assenting to one doctrine and dissenting from the other. Mr. Newman attempts to draw a distinction between the two cases: he asks, is there no difference between adding a word and introducing a doctrine? He says that when the early Christians used the expression " Son of God," they knew what they meant by it. How is it to be shown that they did attach any " pre-
" cise and minute" definition to it. That fact, so simply and so easily assumed by Mr. Newman, is equally incapable of proof

from historical evidence or reasonable supposition; the best historians assure us that, so far from this having been the case, the doctrine of the Trinity had escaped human speculation, till the controversy arose, which was decided at the council of Nice. We have every reason to believe that, before this time, all Christians received the doctrine of the Trinity just as we find it revealed in Scripture, without exploring further into its nature or extent; at all events, such inquiry was confined to private individuals, and the result was never put forth as a necessary article of faith. It is impossible to maintain that the reception of the decision at this council of Nice is necessary to salvation, upon the authority of that council itself, without admitting the complete infallibility of the Church. There is no *via media* between the two propositions. The Church of Rome will not allow that they *added* the doctrine of Transubstantiation. They say that such is the true interpretation of certain texts in

Scripture, and that the orthodox Christians had always so interpreted them; that when they read "This is my body," "*they knew what they meant by it*," and that the doctrine of Transubstantiation contains that meaning. They will tell us that **the authority of the Church was the same in both cases**, exercised in the same manner, and the decision of the Church promulgated by the same means, *viz.*, a General Council. The damnatory clauses cannot be used or applied in Mr. Newman's sense (which I will readily grant was the sense in which they were originally composed), except upon the ground that the Church is an infallible interpreter of Scripture, and that this minute and precise description of the doctrine of the Trinity is her interpretation of it.

Let us now consider Mr. Newman's theory of Church Infallibility, in which he makes a desperate effort to draw a distinction between our infallibility and that of the Church of Rome.

Mr. Newman gives three texts amongst many others as proving the infallibility of the Church; he supposes, that the promise of divine security from error is contained in them. In this one instance he surely would not contend that the Church must be her own interpreter; he never can pretend to adduce certain passages in Scripture to prove the divine gift of true interpretation to the Church, and then make the interpretation which the Church herself puts upon these very passages, binding upon the private Christian for whose conviction they are adduced.

The following are the texts referred to.

" The Church of the living God, the
" pillar and ground of the truth."—" He
" gave some apostles, and some prophets,
" and some evangelists, and some pastors
" and teachers; for the perfecting of the
" saints, for the work of the ministry, for
" the edifying of the body of Christ; till
" we all come in the unity of the faith,
" and of the knowledge of the Son of God

"unto a perfect man, unto the measure of the stature of the fulness of Christ; in order that we be henceforth no more children, tossed to and fro, carried about with every wind of doctrine."—"As for me, this is my covenant with them, saith the Lord; my spirit that is upon thee, and my words which I have put in thy mouth, shall not depart out of thy mouth, nor out of the mouth of thy seed, nor out of the mouth of thy seeds' seed, saith the Lord, from henceforth and for ever."

If these passages amount to a promise of infallibility to the Church, and we so interpret them, how can such interpretation be reconciled with our Nineteenth Article, which distinctly asserts that the various Churches have "erred in matters of faith?" If, on the contrary, we suppose they contain a promise of assistance in preaching the truth, but not divine security from error, it is plain that they will not support Mr. Newman's view of Church authority.

Granting that they *do* contain this promise to the Church, that she should be for ever divinely secured from error, a serious difficulty arises, *viz.*, how we shall sufficiently get rid of the pretensions of the Church of Rome, so as to justify the Reformation and the change of doctrine which resulted from it? This is a difficulty of no ordinary kind to the Oxford Tracts party. It must be evident that the Reformation itself is looked upon by some of them as a sore burden, grievous to be borne, but which must be borne, as long as they continue apparent members of the Established Church. Mr. Froude openly avowed, that "he hated the Reformation more and more," and committed the expression to writing, which his friends published. This is then a very serious difficulty, how to interpret these, and similar passages, so as to support their views of Church infallibility, and yet to excuse their continuing members of our Church.

Mr. Newman says:—

"The texts just quoted are considered
"by the Romanists to prove the infallibi-
"lity of the Church in all matters of faith
"and general morals. They certainly
"will *bear* so to be interpreted, it cannot
"be denied: and if this be so, why, it may
"be asked, do we not interpret them as
"the Romanists do? I answer by referring
"to the parallel of the Mosaic Law?
"God's favour was promised to the Israel-
"ites for ever, but has been withdrawn
"from them. Has God's promise, there-
"fore, failed? or rather, was it not for-
"feited by neglect on the part of his peo-
"ple to perform the conditions on which
"it was granted? Surely we so account
"for the rejection of the nation when
"Christ came. Even supposing, then,
"for argument's sake, that the promises
"to the Christian Church be in themselves
"as ample as the Romanists pretend, per-
"chance they have been since forfeited or
"suspended in their measure by our dis-
"obedience."

He goes on to argue that, as the promises to the Jews were only fulfilled *in part,* so it is the case with the promises to the Church. He sees no reason why it should not have been *intended* that the whole extent of the promises should be fulfilled, but observes, "that all through the " inspired history, *we have traces of the " divine intentions mysteriously frustrated :*" and that " God's promises depend on man's " co-operation with them for their fulfil- " ment *in detail.*" What can Mr. Newman possibly mean when he speaks of the " Divine intentions being mysteriously " *frustrated?*" Can Mr. Newman conceive that it is in the power of man by withholding his " co operation" to *frustrate* the intentions of God? The difficulty above mentioned, is thus to be solved by a rash and unauthorized assumption. First, we must assume that this parallel exists between the Christian Church and the Jews, and then we must assume, that we know the degree in which these promises have been suspended. The promises are said to have been partly forfeited by the breach of unity. How do we know they have not been wholly lost? If these were the conditions and we have broken them, how can we positively assert that we enjoy any part of them? But we are to be justified in departing from the doctrine of the Church of Rome on the presumption that these promises are not fulfilled in detail in consequence of our sins and errors, and then are to be warranted in " holding the " infallibility of the Church, as some di- " vines express it, in matters of saving " faith," upon the ground of these very same promises: and that is not all — we are to judge *how far* they are withdrawn, and to what extent they are continued. We are to assume that they are so far forfeited as to make the Romish Church corrupt, and so far fulfilled as to justify us in condemning those who presume to differ with ourselves.

We are to be enabled to reject the doctrine of Transubstantiation, which had been received for a long time by nearly the whole Christian Church, and then retain a "minute and precise description" of such an awful and mysterious doctrine as that of the Trinity, and assert that, whosoever does not believe and agree to this minute and precise description, "without doubt, "shall perish everlastingly," and we are to do this in the face of so many simple and plain texts as the following :

"Who art thou that judgest another "man's servant; to his own master he "standeth or falleth?"

"Not that we have dominion over your "faith, but are helpers of your joy."

"For where two or three are gathered "together in my name, there am I in the "midst of them."

"For if there be first a willing mind, it "is accepted according to that a man "hath, and not according to that he hath "not."

" Him that is weak in the faith receive
" ye, but not to doubtful disputation."

" Judge not, that ye be not judged:
" for with what judgment ye judge, ye
" shall be judged; and with what measure
" ye mete, it shall be measured to you
" again."

" But with me, it is a very small thing
" that I should be judged of you, or of
" man's judgment."

" Therefore, judge nothing before the
" time, until the Lord come, who both will
" bring to light the hidden things of dark-
" ness, and will make manifest the coun-
" sels of the hearts."

Texts of the same description are far too numerous to quote. Mr. Newman admits that the promises of infallibility to the Church, were given upon the condition of unity: he is compelled to allow that the condition is broken on our part. To maintain any difference at all between himself and the Romish Church, he is also compelled to admit, that the promises are, to a certain extent, forfeited, and the question now is, whether we are to abandon the damnatory clauses, as he explains them, in deference to these numerous, simple, and plain passages in Scripture, or retain them as a proof of holding the infallibility of the Church, upon the strength of a bold and hazardous speculation, that we know to what degree these promises are now fulfilled to the Church. Can we dare to pronounce upon the condition of those who conscientiously differ from the doctrines of our Church upon such a speculation? Are we justified in presuming that these promises of infallibility are fulfilled in that measure and degree exactly, as may suit any " peculiar views" upon the subject?

Again, supposing that this gift of infallibility was bestowed upon the Church, and forfeited, either wholly or in some measure, by any particular act of schism, or at any particular date or period, as Mr. Newman appears to think, it is argued, that an infallible interpretation of Scripture is to be found, if not in the present Church, at least in the Church as it existed previous to that particular date, or great act of schism; it is said that by a reference to what is called Primitive Antiquity, this infallible interpretation can be historically arrived at, and is therefore binding upon our consciences as such. It is admitted that the best divines are divided as to the time when this age of purity ceased; there are strong grounds for supposing that schism, to a great degree, has existed since the time of the Apostles. Who therefore is to decide, without fear of mistake, what number of years or centuries is to be included in this Primitive Antiquity? Who can say, how much of this promised infallibility was forfeited at any particular date? Again, can we ascertain historically, *with a sufficient degree of precision*, what the particular interpretation of certain doctrines absolutely was at that time? Let us remember that our historians on this point are bishops or clergy, who soon assumed much greater powers than they originally had, and who do not appear to have consulted the lay members at all in their decisions about the doctrines of the Church: they would naturally be prejudiced in favour of any doctrine or theory which supported high notions of their spiritual privileges. If we reflect that " the heart is deceitful above all " things," we may justly suspect *ourselves* in any investigation where such privileges are concerned. Dr. Shuttleworth has ably shown how prone both parties, clerical and lay, must be from different motives, to adopt and fall into such a theory: the concession of such privileges on the part of the lay churchmen in those days of darkness and want of education, is by no means a confirmation of the justice with which they were claimed. If *any* doubt exists, surely the safer course is to claim too little than too much; where our right of speaking so peremptorily upon the terms of salvation are not most clear and unequivocal, it must be the wiser and more charitable course to forbear: it must be more in accordance with the whole spirit of the Gospel and the sense of our own errors and imperfections.

Amongst the other numerous inconsistencies in which Mr. Newman has inevitably involved himself in the elucidation of his theory of the true Anglican doctrine, there is one on this point of the Church being divinely secured from error, which I must here mention. In page 241, he says,—

" If this view of the subject be in the
" main correct, it would follow, that the
" ancient Church will be our model in all
" matters of doctrine, till it broke up into
" portions, and for Catholic agreement
" substituted peculiar and local opinions;
" *but that since that time the Church has*
" *possessed no fuller measure of the truth*
" *than we see it has at this day, viz., merely*
" *the fundamental faith.*"

Page 248, we read —

" But whenever the fatal deed took place, it is long done and past, and its effects live to this day. *Century after century the Church Catholic has become more and more disunited, discordant, and corrupt.*"

In the 244th page too, Mr. Newman alludes to a time "*when error was universal.*" These are material and important contradictions in a writer who is endeavouring to support the infallibility of the Church, and that what she teaches is right *because* she teaches it; if the Church is " divinely secured from error," as Mr. Newman asserts, whether that security is said to be complete, or only extended to the " essentials of the gospel," it becomes a most important point to ascertain, whether the Church has gradually become more and more corrupt or not; her gift of infallibility must be seriously involved in such an investigation. The assertor of such infallibility on her behalf, ought to have most clear and decisive views upon the subject. Supposing Mr. Newman to be equally sincere and candid at all times and on all occasions, it must follow, from the quotations I have given, that he has by no means such clear ideas of the state in which the Church now is, or has been, in this respect, since any given date; I do not mean that he cannot actually measure the present amount of the security from error afforded to the Church, for that must be beyond the power of man, but he has no fixed notion of what he himself *thinks* her state to be. His theory has never been "*realized*" even to himself, and it is impossible to allow such a ponderous building as Church infallibility to be erected on such an invisible and indeterminate foundation.

Mr. Newman professes to be a member of the reformed Church: his party complain that they are unjustly accused of hostility to the Reformation. Notwithstanding numerous passages denoting such hostility, they are anxious to maintain their adherence to the principles which were recognized by the Reformation itself; their theological system, as far as it can be ascertained, is, however, totally incompatible with any theory which could justify our separation from Rome. Mr. Newman says:

"Is there any limit to that faith which
"the creed represents? I answer, there
"is no precise limit; nor is it necessary
"that there should be. Let this maxim be
"laid down concerning *all* that the Church
"Catholic holds, to the full extent of her
"prophetical Tradition, that her members
"must either believe or silently acquiesce
"in *the whole* of it. *Though the meaning*
"*of the creed be extended ever so far*, it
"cannot go beyond our duty of obedience,
"if not of active faith; and if the line
"between the creed and the general doc-
"trine of the Church cannot be drawn,
"neither can it be drawn between the
"lively apprehension and submission of
"her members in respect to both the one

" and the other. Whether it be apprehen-
" sion or submission, it is faith in one or
" other shape, nor can individuals them-
" selves distinguish between what they
" spiritually perceive and what they accept
" upon authority. It is the duty of every
" one either to believe and love what he
" hears, or to wish to do so, or, at least, not
" to oppose, but to be silent."

How can a man approve of the Reformation, upon whose theological theory *no* reformation could be justified? If we are bound to believe, or to silently acquiesce in *all* the Church Catholic holds, it is quite certain that no doctrinal reformation could ever properly take place. A doctrinal reformation *must* arise from some one individual, or a number of individuals first *doubting* the truth of a doctrine, then *investigating*, and then *rejecting* it. The infallibility of the Church was held and received; no reformation in any one doctrinal point could possibly be accomplished without absolutely rejecting the tenet of infallibility; but by Mr. Newman's own hypothesis we are not justified in *doubting* about any extension of the creed, much less in *disbelieving* in it. Without therefore considering any other doctrines, such as Transubstantiation and the worship of Images, it is clear that the whole and only principle of the Reformation, consists in the violation of Mr. Newman's rule. Mr. Newman cannot understand his own principles, or he cannot be a consistent member of any reformed Church.

When the question arises where the voice of the Church is to be found, supposing it established that we are bound to obey it in preference to our own interpretation of Scripture, Mr. Newman refers us to our " formularies and services." He says:—

" The daily prayer, the occasional offices,
" the order of the sacraments, the ordina-
" tion services, present one and the same
" strong, plain, edifying language to rich
" and poor, learned and unlearned, and
" that not as the invention of this reformer

" or that, but as the witness of all saints " from the beginning." It may be granted that all our prayers and offices are but selections from writings of the highest antiquity, and that none of them are the invention of this reformer or that, without its affecting the argument attempted to be founded upon such a fact. The *selection* has been dictated by this reformer or that, or many of the reformers together. They rejected every thing which appeared to *them* to militate against pure doctrine. The theological doctrines drawn from such a selection, must consequently depend upon the opinions of the parties who made the selection. The doctrines of the Anglican Church have been altered to a very great extent *since* the separation from Rome and the throwing off the supremacy of the Pope. They may in the next century be again altered or modified, and the virtue of infallibility cannot attach to the voice of the Church, if that voice speaks a totally different language in different centuries. I will mention one passage more in Mr. Newman's book, which is as contrary to our articles and Protestant faith as any I have alluded to.

Mr. Newman says, page 332—

" The last words of the Apocalypse are, " I suppose, the sole great exception to this " remark, the sole declaration in the books " of the New Testament, of an *exclusive* " character; and surely they cannot be " considered sufficient in themselves to " establish so bold and eventful a negative, " *viz.*, that nothing is necessary doctrine " but what is in it." The obvious inference is that, in Mr. Newman's judgment, there *are* necessary doctrines which are *not* contained in the books of the New Testament: which sentiment is quite in accordance with Mr. Keble's declaration, that there was a deposit with the Church " independent of and distinct from the " truths which are directly Scriptural." We have on the one side, according to Mr. Newman, the omission in Scripture of any assertion of its own sufficiency and completeness, and on the other a single assertion, as strong and as plain as it is possible for language to be, that it *is* sufficient. The antecedent presumption that the Scripture would be sufficient and complete, is, *at least*, as strong as the contrary. One distinct assertion must go further to prove the affirmative, than the omission in other places can do to prove the negative. Let us look again to those articles which Mr. Newman has subscribed, which contain the doctrines of a Church to which he *professes* to belong, and the voice of which he strenuously asserts and maintains is to be listened to by us in preference to any opinions of our own. A Church, which he conceives to be divinely secured from error, and infallible in matters of saving faith.

The sixth article says:—

" Holy Scripture containeth all things
" necessary to salvation; so that whatsoever
" is not read therein, or may be proved there-

" by, is not to be required of any man, that i
" should be thought requisite or necessary
" to salvation."

And in the face of this article and in spite of all his high notions of Church authority, Mr. Newman ventures to say, that the assertion " that nothing is necessary doctrine but what is in Holy Scripture," is a " bold and eventful negative."

In the preceding pages I have endeavoured to show some of the numerous inconsistencies and contradictions into which Mr. Newman's opinions have led him. We have seen it advanced by him at one time, that the Scriptures were plain and easy to be understood in all essential matters, that the Church was not infallible, and that following Tradition has led to error: at another time he states, that the Scriptures are so obscure in their principal doctrines that scarcely any person could discover them, that we hold the infallibility of the Church, and that the greatest mistakes have arisen from following Scripture and neglecting Tradition. If we give him credit for sincerity and candour, he appears, through his whole book, to flutter between the tenets of the Church of Rome and those of the Church of England. He seems to differ from Rome not so much in principle as in practice; to agree in their Church infallibility, but not in the use they have made of it; to admit their rule of Tradition, but to differ from them as to what traditions are worthy of adoption. The difference he maintains, may be resolved into one of the individuals who compose the Church at any given time, and the same principle in the hands of other men in a future century may, indeed according to all our knowledge of human nature *must*, lead to the same lamentable results. The principle of Church infallibility, and the denial of the right of private judgment, the setting the Church free from the necessity of appealing to the plain interpretation of Scripture, must inevitably lead, sooner or later, as it has before led, to great profligacy in the clergy, irreligion in the upper classes of the laity, and darkness and superstition amongst the great mass of the people. As long as human nature remains what it is, the same causes will always produce nearly the same effects. Church infallibility is like despotic power in civil government, it avoids many evils, and combines many advantages *when in good hands*, but as that never can be expected long to be the case, it has in the end been found to be as destructive to true religion as despotism is to civil liberty. That the great leaning of the Oxford Tracts is in favour of the tenets of the Romish Church cannot admit of a doubt; I will allow that a few expressions ought not to decide the character of a whole work, or a system: but when a multitude of quotations all strongly tending to the same point are combined with various similar peculiarities in the private opinions of the authors themselves, it is quite fair to deduce from them the character of the whole. The following examples will show the popish tenets of the Oxford Tracts writers.

" I can see no other claim which the
" prayer book has on a layman's deference,
" as the teaching of the Church, which the
" Breviary and the Missal have not *in a far*
" *greater degree.*"

" I should like to know why you flinch
" from saying that the power of *making*
" *the body and blood of Christ* is vested in
" the successors of the Apostles. I am
" more and more indignant at the Pro-
" testant doctrine on the subject of the
" Eucharist, and think that the principle
" on which it is founded, is as proud,
" irreverent, and foolish, as that of any
" heresy, even Socinianism."

" It has lately come into my head that
" the present state of things in England

"makes an opening *for reviving the mo-nastic system.*"

" I think people are injudicious who talk against Roman Catholics for worshipping saints, and honouring the Virgin and images, &c. &c. These things may *perhaps* be idolatrous. I cannot make up my mind about it."

" He hates the *meagreness of Protestantism* as much as either of us."

" That odious Protestantism."

" As to the Reformers, I think worse and worse of them. Jewell was what you would call in these days *an irreverent dissenter.*"

" Why do you praise Ridley? Do you know sufficient good about him to counterbalance the fact that he was *the associate of Cranmer*, Peter Martyr, and Bucer."

" Really I hate the Reformation and the Reformers more and more."

" The Reformation was a limb badly set. It must be broken again in order to be righted."

All the above extracts are from Mr. Froude's Remains. He was one of the principal promoters of the Oxford Tracts, and this volume has been published by two leading persons of the same party, as " A " Witness of Catholic views, and to speak " a word for the Church of God," as declared in their preface to it.

In the Tracts themselves we find Popish doctrines as unequivocally maintained or sanctioned.

" The English Church is, for certain, " deficient in particulars, because it does " not profess itself *infallible*."—Tract 71, p. 27.

" The argument of ultra Protestantism " may be taken, and we may say, 'The " ' Bible, and nothing but the Bible;' but " this is an unthankful rejection of tradi-" tion, another great gift, *equally from* " *God*."—Tract 71, p. 8.

" Scripture and tradition taken together " *are the joint rule of faith*."—Tract 71, p. 2.

"Why should we take upon ourselves to say that they (*the dead* in Christ) who are his members, as well as we, have no interest in this, which is offered as a memorial of all? Or why should men think it an unhappiness or imperfection, *that they should obtain additional joys and satisfactions thereby.*"—Tract 81, p. 7.

"*The primitive practice of praying for the dead.*"

"The Church of England nowhere restrains her Children from praying for their *departed* friends."—Tracts for the Times.

"Grant, O Lord, we beseech thee, that we thy servants may enjoy perpetual health of mind and body, and by *the glorious intercession of the ever-virgin Mary,* may be delivered from present sorrow, and have the fruition of everlasting joy."

"O God, who, when thy Apostle Peter walked on the waves, savedst him from drowning with thy right hand, and thrice delivered his fellow Apostle Paul from "shipwreck on the open sea, favourably hear us, and grant that *by the deserts of them both*, we may obtain everlasting glory."—Tract 75, pp. 80, 81.

"The prevailing notion of *bringing forward the atonement* explicitly and prominently on all occasions, is evidently quite opposed to what we consider the teaching of Scripture; nor do we find any sanction for it in the Gospels. If the Epistles of St. Paul appear to favour it, it is only at first sight."—Tract 80, p. 74.

"The *(so called)* Reformers."—Tract 38, p. 74.

"The English Church, as such, is *not Protestant,* only politically, that is externally."—Tract 71, p. 32.

Innumerable passages could be found, all manifestly tending in one and the same direction; all showing a departure from the known and avowed principles of the Church of England, and the adoption of those of the Church of Rome. The expressions are far too plain and unequivocal to admit of more than one direct and obvious sense. If any defence is to be raised upon the fact of their being misunderstood or misinterpreted, weak as such a defence must be, it ought to be recollected that the very object of these tracts, and of other separate publications of their authors, is declared to be to *bring out and make apparent what the true Anglican doctrine is.* The Anglican theology is said not to have been hitherto "*realized,*" or brought home to the mind. The Oxford Tracts party profess that their labours are directed to supply this great deficiency in our Church system. They purpose to set before us in their true light, what the doctrines of our own Church really are. They find no fault with our articles, they only desire to explain them to us properly. It must be evident, that if on any one occasion the least ambiguity of expression is unpardonable, it must be on this, as ambiguity and uncertainty are themselves the very defects to be remedied. The particular situation of these individuals must also be taken into account. They are high in authority in one of our Universities, their peculiar office is to direct the studies and prepare the minds of nearly half the young men of our nation, who are intending to take orders in our Church; their influence over them must be very great; when the passions are warm and the judgment weak, how little are they able to counteract any erroneous impressions which may be made upon them! At such a time the greatest possible caution ought to be exercised. All mistake and misconstruction ought to be strictly guarded against, and upon the most vital doctrines of our Church, ambiguity is nearly as bad as error.

In a great many of their general sentiments upon the Roman Catholic Church, I believe them to be correct. Attached as I am to Protestantism in its strongest sense, I never could hear the Roman Catholic ceremonies, or dress, &c. spoken of as mummeries or fopperies, without pain. We ought to remember that our kneeling at prayer, and our clergy wearing a surplice or bands, are precisely the same in kind, and may as justly be spoken of in the same terms by those who choose to consider them in that light. The Roman Catholics may multiply forms and ceremonies to a great degree, and thus draw men's minds from the realities of religion; they may appeal strongly to the imagination and but little to the reason, but it can never be right or necessary to speak of such an error, if it is one, in terms of ridicule or scorn. The evangelical party would do well to recollect that they are themselves running into the only error worth contending against in the Romish Church: the error which is the root and foundation of all the rest, *viz.* an assumption of infallibility. Church infallibility is bad enough, but *personal* infallibility is much worse; and whenever we presume to condemn those who differ from us in such violent and unlimited terms, we are in effect and reality setting ourselves up as *judges* upon the religious opinions and observances of our fellow Christians. It is curious enough that many men, who are most violent against the Roman Catholics and the Oxford Tracts party, practically are as tenacious of the same authority they profess to decry, when exercised in the support of their own religious opinions. It is too common to hear the Protestant Dissenters spoken of as sinners and schismatics, inasmuch as they have separated themselves from the Established Church. That they *may* be schismatics, and so far sinners, is very certain, but I could never understand how we can take upon ourselves to *decide* that point, without assuming the same principle of Church infallibility, which we deny to the Church of Rome. How can we avail ourselves of any right at one time, and deny the exercise of it to others at another? Great efforts have been made to show that the Reformation was not such as it is commonly represented: it has been argued, that all we did was to go back to the original faith and doctrine established in this country before the Church of Rome overpowered us: that we merely cast off her chains and regained our liberty, and that the separation of Protestant Dissenters from our own Church now, bears no analogy to our departing from Rome then. One great difference in the two cases there certainly is, the Romish faith *was* the religion of the State; at the Reformation it ceased to be so, and the present Established Church took its place. If there is any obligation upon our consciences to accede to those religious opinions which the State may adopt, we may or rather must be right, and the Roman Catholics and Protestant Dissenters equally wrong; but if this is really so, it must inevitably follow, that should the State revert to the Roman Catholic faith, we shall be obliged in conscience to follow its example. This theory surely can find few advocates, and yet upon what other grounds can Dr. Hook assert that the Roman Catholics are schismatics in England, and members of a true branch of the Church of Christ in France? Supposing that we are *not* bound by the religious principles which the State may happen to adopt, there are some weighty considerations which should induce us to pause before we presume to condemn or judge either the Roman Catholics or the Protestant Dissenters. We will admit that our Church was for many centuries held in bondage by the Church of Rome, supported by the civil power in those ages. A combination of circumstances enabled us to cast off this heavy yoke. All power of the Pope in matters of religion in this country was denied. Henry the Eighth was declared the supreme head of the Church; religious liberty was obtained as far as Rome was concerned; and a convocation was held, at which Articles of Religion were agreed upon; they were signed by our two Archbishops, and about nineteen Bishops, and numerous members of high station in the Church. But what was the tenour of these articles? Were they identical with those now in use in this same Anglican Church? By no means. They explicitly recognized the seven sacraments of the Church of Rome. The doctrine of Penance and Transubstantiation were explained and enforced. In short, the only material difference between the Anglican and Romish Churches in that day, was putting Henry the Eighth in the place previously occupied by the Pope. It may be true enough to assert, that although the authority of the Church of Rome was abrogated, her influence to a great extent remained; it may justly be said that the reformers themselves could hardly be expected to shake off all their old opinions at once: that early habit and association would, to a certain degree, prevent them from arriving at the simple truth on many doctrinal points; that the will of the Sovereign, at that time so far more influential than at present, may have cramped their deliberations, which would otherwise have been conducted in a different manner, and led to a different conclusion. But how can we *know* or *decide* absolutely that these same causes may not in a degree have operated when our present articles and religious constitution was settled and agreed upon? How can we *know* that the influence of Popery was then entirely extinct? The lapse of time since any alteration has taken place is by no means so strong an argument as may be supposed. When the civil power, either with or without the advice or concurrence of the Church itself, promulgates certain articles of faith, and then renders a subscription to those articles, and an agreement upon doctrinal points in them absolutely necessary in the clergy, there is a good deal, even without the use of any external force, to secure their adoption independent of their truth and accordance with Scripture. As a matter of course, all the honours and emoluments of the clerical profession are then to be obtained on these terms alone. The absolute nomination of bishops has been vested in the state, and the state would certainly make choice of those persons who favoured its views, and would sign and support these articles: this would influence the whole Church down to the lowest member of it. A vast proportion of the talent of the country would be enlisted on this side; in the education of youth, which is so much in the hands of the clergy, those theological works would principally be used, which would, as it is called, give an *orthodox* explanation of these particular points. Early impressions and prejudices would be created, and assist in promoting the continuance of these religious tenets. It is certainly very possible that individuals might on further examination disapprove of some of them; but let us consider the situation in which they would be placed, and how far it would operate in discouraging such a disapprobation, or the avowal of it. The laity, as a body, seldom devote much of their time to the investigation of abstruse theological doctrines, so it will be only necessary to regard the clergy. At the time of life when the Church is chosen as a profession, and these articles are to be subscribed, and these tenets to be embraced, it is absolutely impossible that a fair judgment can be arrived at. If they are conscientiously subscribed at all, it must be, to a very great extent, upon the credit of the Church for the time being. Many never renew their investigation; and most of those who do, from all these powerful influences, only confirm their previous decision. Paley has said, that whoever attacks a flourishing establishment, writes with a halter about his neck. Where civil liberty exists, this can never be positively true, but it may be negatively so. Take the case of a man who finds himself in the Church, in the enjoyment of a competency in it, having relinquished all prospects in any other profession—his fortune, if he had any, having been perhaps spent in his education, or in the acquisition of his preferment in the Church;—before he has had time to give his mature consideration, which can only be done at a mature age, to these doctrinal points, he finds that his bread depends upon his forming a certain decision about them. He finds, that if from any cause he cannot conscientiously continue a member of that Church from which his provision is derived, he must turn out upon the world, with probably a wife and family who can take no part in the discussion, without an income and without a home. It must be quite obvious, that supposing there was any doctrinal error contained in our articles, or religious tenets, it might easily go on for centuries without correction. The few who discerned such error would have the strongest possible inducements to keep their discoveries to themselves. Now it may be asked why the decision of the Church, in the time of Edward the Sixth, was *neces-*

sarily more correct than in the time of Henry the Eighth upon doctrinal points? If the reason given is, that the influences of Popery were then considerably decreased and worn away, it must by implication suggest the *possibility* of those influences not being entirely extinguished even now. If it be said that such later decision is more in accordance with Scripture or antiquity, the *possibility* that some future generation *may* arrive at a determination of these very points still nearer to the Scriptures and antiquity, must obviously occur to us. In short, no answer can be given upon the subject, which would not quite put aside the assumption of infallibility for our Church, or such a degree of authority as would alone justify us in *condemning* those who differ from her doctrines. This argument does not rest on mere hypothesis. If an administration, which now stands in the same relation to the Church that the Crown did to it in Henry the Eighth's time, if an administration, I say, greatly favourable to some particular views on certain points of doctrine, should remain in power long enough to fill the bench of Bishops with men attached to their opinions, there is no doubt but that by degrees the views of the whole Church might be affected by it. What is to prevent, in the next century, a revision and material alteration in our Articles or Liturgy? Should such be the case, would the private Christian be bound in conscience to acquiesce in such altered views, or to adhere to those of the time of Henry the Eighth or Edward the Sixth?—all three being materially different to each other on many vital points? Hoadly, and Watson, and Paley, have regarded the subject more or less in the same light, and have thereby drawn down upon themselves the most violent abuse from what has been called the High Church party; but that is no proof that they were in consequence mistaken. Hoadly and Watson have been accused of being Socinians, and Paley is frequently represented as a man of loose religious principles. They are called Latitudinarians, and are constantly represented as advancing, that whatever religious belief a man arrived at in accordance with his conscience, must be right to *him*, and that consequently a right apprehension of particular doctrines is not necessary to salvation. Such accusations result from an ignorant misinterpretation of their true sentiments; they are grounded upon the assumption, that because they deny the infallibility of the Church, they assert and maintain the infallibility of individuals; that because they do not feel authorized in pronouncing sentence against their fellow Christian, on account of his not agreeing with themselves on all doctrinal points, that they therefore hold that these doctrinal points are of no real importance; that because they admitted their own liability to error, and by parity of reasoning that of the Church of their day, they therefore did not feel convinced of the truth of the doctrines of their Church, and those which they themselves professed.

The censures upon these able and excellent men are founded upon a complete confusion between religious charity and humility and the not judging another man's servant on the one hand, and the latitudinarianism which makes no distinction between religious truth and error upon the other; the mistaking freedom of religious opinions, the attendant upon civil liberty, for a licence to religious indifference, and the identifying independence of human authority in religion, with exemption from responsibility to God for our belief. It is very easy to deny assertions which have never been made, or to overthrow positions which have never been taken, but the very course pursued by the High Church party has been a tacit acknowledgment of their inability to cope with the real question at issue. Whether we assume the infallibility of the Church or not in so many words signifies little, but if we act, and think, and speak, as if we really had assumed it, there will be no chance of our establishing a difference between the Church of Rome and ourselves. It will be merely this, that we consider that *we* must be infallible because we are right, and that they are *not* infallible because they are wrong. Far be it from me to excuse any lukewarmness, or want of zeal, in the promotion of what we conscientiously believe to be Christian truth, but the most strenuous efforts in that way are quite consistent with the most perfect charity towards those who differ from us, and the total abstinence from *pronouncing judgment* upon them, under the pretended sanction of Church authority. We may solicit their earnest attention to any points we think necessary, we may warn them of the danger of neglecting or mistaking them, we may exert our whole influence and abilities in making them sensible of what we believe to be their error, but a distrust of our own abilities to decide peremptorily on such occasions will be of more service to us than any multiplication of damnatory clauses or anathemas. Our moderation will have more effect than our denunciations, our charity will make more conversions than our condemnation. One bad effect has always attended, and must ever attend, upon harsh and positive assertions upon matters of doctrine, under the name of contending for the faith, *viz.* the drawing off the minds of men from the necessity of a pure and a holy life to the far easier task of *professing the orthodox faith*. Human nature is glad enough to avoid difficulty and self-denial, and the signing certain articles, attaching ourselves to a certain Church, or supporting particular views of doctrine, requires much less exertion than the reforming our lives and manners. That every effort ought to be made to promote true and correct views of doctrine, is very certain, but any form of Christianity, if sincerely embraced, is surely better than no religion at all; and though the existence of Popery or Dissent may be much regretted, the prevalence of vice and profligacy is immeasurably more to be lamented, and we should be far better employed in endeavouring to educate the young and reclaiming the old, than in setting up and establishing extreme views of the authority of our own particular Church. It may be beyond our abilities in this day to define the limits of the true Church, or to explain the extent of the authority she possesses; nothing is more easy than to interpret passages in Scripture so as to suit our own religious principles, nothing, in short, more simple than to call other Churches Romish, Calvinistic, Arminian, or Lutheran, and our own Scriptural; but the misfortune is that each separate Church has done the same for itself, and this fact alone, together with a due reflection on the numerous causes which may interfere with, and prejudice our judgment, should lead us to put forth our claims with moderation and humility. The theory advanced by Mr. Newman and the writers of the Oxford Tracts, is totally incompatible with their own avowed principles. They themselves by no means submit to that very voice of the Church, which they wish to force upon all other people.

Let them take the sense of the clergy of their own Church, or that of the clergy and laity jointly: or, if they prefer it, that of all the persons whom *they* would admit to be clergy, or members of the true Church; in short, they shall name their own tribunal: they shall then ask for an interpretation of Scripture. All we shall require of them will be that they should, in justice to their own principles, at once sacrifice their private judgment to the decision they may obtain. Whether this Council be composed of members of our own Church, or of those of all other Churches collectively, in whatever conceivable mode it can be selected, it is impossible to imagine that its decree would " realize" "this peculiar development of " feeling" at Oxford. After passing through such an ordeal, Mr. Newman and his party might come out Roman Catholics, Ultra Protestants, or Moderate Churchmen; they could never retain the position they are in at present. It is admitted that they are but a "small remnant" of our own Church, the majority must be increased against them by any addition from without. In which direction they would have to move would depend on the choice they made of their judges; they go too far for us, and the Roman Catholics would make them go a little further. If the Romanists were satisfied, which I imagine they would *nearly* be, it would at all events prove that the Oxford Tracts writers cannot be true Protestants, or consistent members of the reformed Church of England.

The Oxford Tracts have obtained great celebrity, and the propagation of these " peculiar tenets" has been assisted by the supposed learning, abilities, and piety of those who hold them. This celebrity, however, *may* be owing to the startling opinions put forth, and religious tenets of the most opposite kinds have been supported by at least equal learning, abilities, and piety.

Holiness of life is no guarantee for purity of doctrine. The Roman Catholic Fenelon, and the Unitarian Cappe, as far as the human eye can discern, were men as devoted to God as any one of this party can be. Great learning does not necessarily include great abilities. The one implies an extensive collection of materials, the other, the proper arrangement and use of them; and without the latter, the former is but a blind guide. The preface to Mr. Froude's Remains identifies his sentiments with those of his friends, and a fair estimate may be formed of their judgment by what they thought so deserving of publication. The following are a few more extracts from that work.

"As pleasure does not seem to be lessened by the impediments to gratification, so neither wisdom is advanced by the facilities of obtaining knowledge. Knowledge which is put in our way does as little affect our character, as gratifications which are untoiled for do touch our affections."

"They therefore do as much err who assert that what facilitates r ligious instruction does certainly tend to make men better, as he who should require deviation from the scheme of nature whenever this might multiply the instruments of pleasure." Page 75.

"It is curious to observe how every one out here, planters, parsons, and all, have eaten dirt, and fallen into the anti-slavery cant!" Page 348.

"There is something so unpleasing about the niggers, that they spoil the scenery altogether. The thing that strikes me in the cut of these *niggers* is their excessive immodesty, a sort of

" froward stupid familiarity, *intended for
" civility*, which prejudices me against
" them even worse than *Buxton's cant*
" did." Page 355.

" I can't get over my prejudices against
" these *niggers;* every one I meet seems
" to me like an *incarnation* of the whole
" Anti-Slavery Society, and Fowell Bux-
" ton at their head." Page 377.

" I feel it a kind of *duty to sustain in
" my mind an habitual hostility to the nig-
" gers*, and to chuckle over the failures of
" the new system. These wretches con-
" centrate all the whiggery, *dissent, cant,*
" and *abomination* that have been ranged
" on their side." Page 382.

" I see no reason why we should sup-
" pose that the Apostles were in any other
" sort conscious of the influence that
" directed them, than *Bishop Butler was
" when he composed the Analogy, or that the
" inspiration which dictated the sacred writ-
" ings and the work in question (the Ana-

"*logy) differed at all in kind, or very much
"*in degree.*" Page 124.

My first impression on reading these and innumerable other passages, was that they *must* be, as Dr. Hook says, " garbled " extracts and anonymous representa-" tions." On finding them correct quotations, I hoped they might find some excuse in the thoughtless flippancy of a young and sanguine person; and I was astonished at the injustice which might be done to him by their publication : but these very friends, who publish this book, tell us in their preface, that —

" Those who would be fain to account
" his sentences, so direct, fearless, and
" pungent concerning all sorts of men
" and things, as speeches uttered at ran-
" dom, more for present point and effect
" than to declare the speaker's real opi-
" nion, must be met with a denial of the
" fact. The expressions in question were
" not uttered at random; he was not in

"the habit of so speaking. On the other
"hand, speaking to different persons at
"different times, he constantly employed
"the same illustrations and arguments,
"very often the same words. Right or
"wrong, therefore, they were *deliberate*
"opinions; and as he was naturally and
"in principle a downright speaker, *his*
"*words may, in general, be taken more lite-*
"*rally than those of other men.*"

Mr. Froude is now no more, and *de mortuis nil nisi bonum* protects him from harsh criticism. But what can we think of the party who publish such remarks, adopt such sentiments, or share with him in such feelings? In the avowal of popish tenets and hostility to the Reformation, Mr. Froude was clear and undisguised, and in two most material points his views wonderfully coincide with those of the Roman Catholics. First in his disinclination *on principle* to promote religious education, and secondly in his endeavours to spread his popish doctrines by *subtle* and *disguised* means. He writes, "The cultivation of right principles seems to have a tendency to make men dull and stupid." He speaks of "poisoning the minds of the natives, and writing *ad captandum*." "So that one should have no chance of proceeding on the undermining system." Page 321. Biography is said to be the best means " of infusing principles against the reader's will."

In short, let any candid person read Mr. Froude's remains through, with the preface by this very party, and then let him seriously ask himself whether they are justly suspected of Romanism or not? Let him consider how far they are able or proper instructors for intended ministers of the Anglican Church. Was such a writer, or are such editors, competent to undertake the important task of " realizing" our Anglican Theology? If Romanism and Ultra Protestantism are the Scylla and Charybdis of our Church, are such pilots to be trusted to steer the vessel through

in safety? Is this " peculiar develop-
" ment of feeling" really to be depended
upon as constituting the true *via media*
so much sought after and so difficult
to obtain? Mr. Froude says of himself
(and his are *not* random expressions, they
are to be taken to the letter):—" My
" annoyance, whenever I am worsted in
" argument, shows me *that theories of my*
" *own and not the word of God*, are the
" rules on which I act," and the great
body of Protestants have ample reason
to fear that Mr. Froude's friends and
fellow-labourers are following theories of
their own, and not the word of God, and
are " teaching for doctrines the command-
" ments of men."

Lately published, by the same Author,

A DEFENCE

OF

PALEY'S MORAL PHILOSOPHY,

IN ANSWER TO THE OBJECTIONS OF MR. WHEWELL AND PROFESSOR SEDGWICK.

SECOND EDITION.

Price 4s.

THE NEW POOR LAW JUSTIFIED,

WITH

SUGGESTIONS FOR THE ESTABLISHMENT

OF

INSURANCE OFFICES FOR THE POOR.

SECOND EDITION.

Price 1s.

www.ingramcontent.com/pod-product-compliance
Lightning Source LLC
Chambersburg PA
CBHW081324090426
42737CB00017B/3028